Raw Materials

Jen Selinsky

*Not every work included in this book is dated in chronological order. This is not an oversight on my part. Rather, I have made some changes and substitutions.

-J.L.S.

Winter Dreamscape

The month of December may not be my favorite of all the twelve, but there is something I find admirable. The pure richness of the frosty winter snow. There is a place imaginable about the woods in my backyard. A whole new land opens up to us all. Joy is in hearts, alike, during this month.

Outside, in the backyard, there are many paths to choose. One long and meandering, as I hear the fallen leaves crunch underneath my feet. The other is completely covered with snow that is up to the knees of my pants. It burns and soothes, as it is cold.

Children riding sleds on the hill up above with the innocent laughter that I once knew. Faces are bundled up along with boots, coats, and scarves. The laughter is that of a mystic sound, as I walk on to the left of me.

Fine snow falls down, as more of the peaceful white trail reveals itself, as snow descends from my feet as I walk. The woods during the winter have a beautiful meaning of poetry in my eyes that reflect back to my mind.

Cold wind from the skies gently blows against me as I walk on through the misty paths.

Trees seem to call out my name as the heavens above send down more wonder. I ascend from the woods with a great feeling of optimism that the white messengers from heaven are watching over me. The sky in which I look up in is as white, as if it were entirely filled with the lightest clouds.

A walk into civilization is mysterious, being that I am alone. The neighborhood houses seem empty and somewhat desolate from my location and state of mind.

The violent blowing wind is healing to my head, which is weary from the journey. This is the best part, as my heart is filled with joy from the lonely meanderings that stick to my mind.

In the distance, I hear more laughter, as a young couple comes forth, and I soon realize that others are around.

As I wander farther, I smell the richness of delightful food from a window yonder. The happiness of the family above reminds me with their graceful smiles that it is Christmas Day! I turn around and walk in the other direction.

9/4/96

Where I Spend My Time

The general scene of my bedroom is quite elaborate to the witnessing eye. There are so many things that one could break down and comprehend.

My green, painted walls contain posters of those who inspired me, and minor pieces of artwork that have been done.

These are loud and awkward things that express themselves while upward hanging in my room. Noisy blacks, reds, and oranges are seen scattered about in myriads.

A sense of joy and amusement is in my mind, as I look up at Jim Morrison, Jimi Hendrix, and Dave Grohl. The Canadian maple leaf bandana is up with pride, though not part of my nationality.

Feast your eyes on my wooden shelf that is posted just above my stereo. It can stimulate any imagination, as its contents are seen with awe.

Figures of children in dressy attire, horses, cats, musical boxes, and people of all kinds. A whole collaboration of figurines looks like a standing congregation.

Below, there stand clay figures of different sorts. Blue, and red, and pink bears seem as if ready to dance to the music that I presently have playing on the stereo.

The others seem lifeless, but, yet have a story to tell. A decorated, miniature tree sits on the left hand (positioned) speaker, and the birds sway to the wind entering from outside.

My favorite wonder of the room is an abandoned doll house that is now used for a bookshelf. The middle portion of most of my books face outward, as one could look at the title and author. Different colors are seen, as that tugs at my curiosity.

I look at the titles; some in red, and some in white. Willa Cather, Mark Twain, and Rudyard Kipling, *Ivanhoe*, and a book of collected poems, all stare back at me in the face.

I then look to the top and see the large doll that I received as a gift five years ago. That represents a sense of motivation, as I smell of the literary rose.

Behold the wonders of my bedroom, my "leisure quarter," for this may be the last time that anyone may ever see.

9/9/96

Freedom Runs

I wonder what I am doing here, as many different assortments of green trees, colored houses, and white clouds zoom by my eyes in a fast and intense manner. Some loose leaves fall free from the close-by maple trees and into my face, temporarily blinding me for a moment.

My clumsy feet then trip and stumble and carry the rest of me down with them. I rise to see that the knees of my blue jeans are slightly stained with a little muddy dirt. My mind then disregards the fact, as the acute pain on my scratched elbows diminishes.

The sound of the robin is piercing in an elaborate and pulsating manner, as it crescendos back and forth. Swarms of them fly overhead in the other direction as I look up into the sky and see lightly brown colored feathers. A hungry cat spies a fallen robin that has injured its wing. I go by faster.

Cars zoom by me as the bewildered passengers point and stare. There are many different people, and some pets, as I see a white Plymouth, a red Pontiac, and a blue

Mustang. A lot of music is played for an instantaneous second.

Some is to my liking, and the other portion is not. The bass on a few stereo systems is similar to that of a throbbing heart that sounds in agony and pain, but the four guys I spy in the red Trans Am are enthralled by the music. After the red stop sign, the car punches it down and skids on down the road, like that of a roller coaster cart. My running is slowing as I grow weary.

Up further is the sound of children laughing in ignorant and playful tones. They are playing hopscotch in the middle of the road. The bright colors of the stripped skirts and solid pants are not coming closer to my vision. As I run by in a huff, starting to taste the hunger and dehydration, I simply ignore the plain expressions on their wan little faces. Now this run seems insignificant.

I breeze by several neighbors' houses, which have different kinds of dogs that are tied up to their leashes. Some tend to growl and bark as I hurriedly run by. Others probably have the temptation to run with me, as the wolves wander free in the forest.

It is said, now, that I have seen the usual in my small journey outside. No longer will I have the desire to run that great distance in such a short period of time. One can actually feel my heart throbbing and see tears (from the dust on the road) streaming down my eyes. Some may ask what it is that I am running from.

I could smile and simply reply, "Back from the clutches of corruption."

9/10/96

A Whole New Emotion

A silent, starry atmosphere is seen throughout the horizon, as many early observers awake. Shades of the dark blue sky have not rearranged to that of a lighter hue. One can see some brilliant stars off in the outer space of the galaxy, as they commence to diminish and fade. They will not be seen until the following night.

Dewdrops are forming on the firmly closed flowers and the greenest of grass. Fat little drops of clear dew are forming and falling onto a green, wet surface. It is cold. A tickling feeling comes about on the skin when one goes out barefoot, and the dew touches them. The night is waning.

Over yonder in the east, the sun is commencing to rise.

"Look! Look!" the old man across the street says. "Look, you, and greet the day!" He clicks his heels and runs into the house to wake his wife.

The majority of the neighborhood is still fast asleep.

A sky of tainted light blue is turned into a friendly yellow and orange. Pastel colors are forming in the sky that was, hours ago, dark blue. Everything is like a painting, as it turns to suit the dawning of the day.

The sky is described as poetry as children begin to wake.

People around the world rejoice, as the massive ball of warmth and joy is first seen in the skies for that day. Dogs and cats roam around the streets.

No one that I know has told me of despising the break of dawn, for it is such a wonderful sight within itself. Songs from all over the world are sung in the morning to glorify the sun.

It is like a lost language that people recite with tongues of grateful praise, to get words flowing from the coy mouths of those who never seem to say very much at all. A silent prayer, or one that is said out loud, is the hidden language of thought that flows as smoothly as words, when one sees the sun for the very first time, or in the morning when it is glorified.

Over the horizon, the light blue is completely gone. A brilliant and beautiful orange covers the entire sky.

People scream and shout out praise, as another day is present. All problems are forgotten for a brief time, when the sun has risen, until the highest point at noon.

How beautiful and majestic the sunrise has to be for so many of those wonderful emotions to repeat in chorus from day to day.

*previously published in volume XXVI of *The Raider Review*, 1997

10/10/96

Pure Freedom

As I am running, I feel that there is nothing which can stop me! My legs are made of iron, and my system is going smooth, like a car engine, only vastly improved.

There are many people who like to spend their day doing nothing, but I could not live with myself if I felt that way.

I have to feel the wind through my hair, the breeze on my skin, even the sweat pooling down in beads to cool me off is in itself a reward for my hard work.

There is nothing greater than feasting my eyes on God's beauty as I get to look at all the colors coming at me at speeds which can go by quite fast but still allows me to enjoy all the splendor.

On days which are not quite as nice, I am forced to exercise indoors, which is very dull, to say the least. Even looking out the window of my small exercise room does not do it for me because I need space. I need to feel, see, hear, and even smell the fresh air as I am thankful for another day.

My body is my temple, and I am very blessed to be able to use it to function beyond basic means.

People try to talk to me as I am running, and usually, I give a friendly wave, acknowledging their gesture.

Most of the time, however, music is pumping through my ears, enhancing the experience even further!

When I am running, I answer to no man! I am one with God and nature, and I enjoy my surroundings. I am an iron fortress, and nothing can stand in my way.

The reason why it is so difficult to exercise while indoors also is the fact that my exercise space is quite small. I do not have much—no fancy CGI exercise programs or video game systems or equipment. What little view I get from the window is not enough to make me feel alive while I am working on myself.

Running is me expressing pure poetry without having to say a word. The wind and the songs of nature set off a perfect harmony. Even though I have my earphones most of the time, I still like to go outside on walks to hear the wonderful tunes which nature has to provide, oftentimes at dawn or dusk, when this part of the world readies itself for another transition.

Most people would say that this is a waste of time, writing out all my feelings, (and I am not much of a writer) but if anyone who reads this gets to feel the same joy that I feel when experiencing an outdoor run, then all of this was worth it. So, without any further ado, I am off to my next destination. Where is that, you may ask; I'm going in whatever direction the wind is blowing.

9/30/14

Birthday

My thirty-sixth birthday celebration was terrific, and I had a great, few days. The festivities started when Travis and I met his parents at the Cast Iron Grill steakhouse—one of my new favorites. We enjoyed some great food while some classic rock was played on the radio—good tunage. We even met one of the young staff, who also went to the Paul McCartney conccrt!

After we had eaten what we wanted to and boxed the leftovers, the waitress had come out with a surprise—my mother-in-law told her that it was my birthday! Since I got to choose my dessert, I picked the ice cream brownie. I was still full from dinner, so I found it a little difficult to finish the dish, even with some help from Travis, but I did manage.

We had returned to his parents' house shortly after. Moments later, I started opening my gifts. I had received many great things, including some lotion, body wash, pajamas, comfy slippers, an Amazon gift card, one for Longhorn, and a John Lennon T-shirt. Travis's aunt also left a gift for me—a foot pampering kit.

And, if all that spoiled me enough, one of the greatest surprises of the evening came from a TV. My mother-in-law had me close my eyes and see if I could guess what she was putting on. As soon as I heard the music, I knew that it had something to do with Genesis!

I opened my eyes to see that she had put on their new documentary.

Travis had not known about this much ahead of time, so we were, as our English friends would say, chuffed!

All four or us enjoyed the documentary, but Travis and I were disappointed that they didn't include Steve Hackett very much, as he is a very underrated talent. Hopefully, the DVD copy will include more footage on him.

We let our food settle as we watched that, and I enjoyed every minute of the documentary. I cannot wait until we can get our own copy.

Next up was the cake, with copious amounts of vanilla ice cream. Margie made the cake, and it tasted every bit as delicious as Bobbi's.

The portions we had taken home are in the fridge right now; I look forward to enjoying those later.

By the time we got home, it was after midnight. I went ahead and changed a few of the clocks after I called Mom and told her about my evening.

Even though I had yet to wake up on the next day, it was still after 12:00, so I thought I would open a few more of my gifts. The first was from my good friend, Chris, in Australia. I opened the card first, which was lovely, as I especially liked the message about her wishing that she was with me. The gifts were wrapped together, so I pulled the first one out which was on top. It was a packet of body lotions, which was nice because I can use them this time of year. Also enclosed was Nora Roberts' new book, *Blood Magyk*. Although I've only read two of her books before, I'm looking forward to this one.

Next were three of Travis's gifts, one of which was a new *TMNT* shirt, faded black with the classic faces. As soon as I took it out of the bag, I knew that I was going to wear it. Next was the Blu-ray version of *A Million Ways to Die in the West*, which I had been curious about for a while. The third was one I was expecting, *Sylvia Plath's*

Drawings, published under Frieda Hughes. I was happy with these gifts and decided to wait until after dinner to open the others.

I woke up early in the afternoon and played on the computer until it was time to rouse Travis. Of course, we had gone to Cheddar's as planned.

They must have known that we were coming because they played "Easy Lover" by Phil Collins and "Sledghammer" by Peter Gabriel. So I sat there in my *TMNT* shirt and sunglasses, singing along to "Sledgehammer" at an audible volume. I didn't care, though, because it was my birthday!

Later, "Heartache Tonight" came on, and I sang part of it in the ladies' room, even though there was someone else in there. It wasn't as bad as it sounds, because I was only washing my hands.

Dinner was good, but the restaurant was getting crowded. It was good we left when we did because more people had started to come in.

When we got home, I opened my remaining gifts. One was *Willy Wonka and the Chocolate Factory* on Blu-ray. The next one was a Doors documentary called *Doors*

R-Evolution. The third physical gift was *Teenage Mutant Ninja Turtles: The Ultimate Visual History.*

Downstairs, Travis revealed his final gift, *Duran Duran Unstaged* on Amazon Prime! I decided we would watch that after *A Million Ways to Die in the West.* All in all, I had a great two days!

11/3/14

Breaking Free

I am always happy for people when they get to leave this library. The older folks are lucky because, oftentimes, they get to retire. The younger ones, though they are simply changing work locations, still have the advantage of leaving. To me, that means they will be much happier where they are going.

I'm very fortunate to have been offered my job in early 2005. The phone interview took place on January 31 of that year, and I was hired immediately. The director at the time and I agreed on a start date of March 1, 2005.

Even though I've always hated work, I couldn't be more excited. I was finally moving out of the congested Cranberry Township, Pennsylvania to a little town called Sellersburg, located in southern Indiana. I would get a chance to live the rest of my life somewhere different and exciting.

I'd given my two weeks' notice at Lone Star, but there was something more difficult that I had to do before I left Cranberry; I had to break things off with my boyfriend of nearly three years. I felt bad about having to do that.

Our lives were heading in different directions.

He wanted to get married and have children, and I wanted nothing to do with that!

I'd also wanted to get out of Pennsylvania, so here was the perfect opportunity to do so.

During the month of February, I'd already started to imagine what my new life was going to be like. Thanks to my job, I was able to start saving money, but that was not even the best part.

In late July 2005, I met the man of my dreams online.

Two months later, we had our first date. We met and had dinner at the Cracker Barrel in Sellersburg and went to the Green Tree Mall in Clarksville. Things only seemed to go uphill from there.

Travis and I knew that we wanted to get married someday, and that day came nearly three years later, when we moved into our new home together.

Now that the mortgage is nearly paid off, I am grateful because of the fact that I've had this job to help finance everything. I have also been able to keep some money in the savings accounts.

But, having been in that library for a decade makes me feel like I've already been there too long. Many times had I became frustrated with my job—cursing obscenities and telling everyone how badly I want to leave. I am also concentrating on my writing during most of my leisure time, and I hope to complete and finalize all my work soon—well as soon as reasonable!

There has been a fair amount of turnover in the staff since I've started. People have left for other jobs, retired, and changed positions. Lots of staff have been hired since I've started—one person even came and left twice. And while I don't envy those who've left for new jobs, because they still have to work, it still feels like a victory, at least to me.   They've gotten to leave that place. Someday, this institution will have a claim on me no more!

I know that I should be grateful and not complain about my job, but I'm only human. I shall have my reward, but all in God's time. Whenever He deems worthy for me to leave, I will get to do so.

Besides, I still get to do what I love, even though I can't make a living from it…yet. At least I've had this solid, well-paying job, which provides part of what I need, all through the Good Lord's bounty!

12/19/14

There must have been many times in my life when I said that I'm going to quit writing altogether. I was burnt out and determined to hang up my pen once and for all. It was time to make way for all those who were just starting off with something of their own to say.

One can guess how many successful attempts that I've had at this, and zero would be the correct answer! The only time that I've come relatively close was in 2010, where I went nearly seven months without writing anything, except what was required for work. After that came a literal explosion of words. I'd gone back to poetry and prose, and my angry muse returned with a vengeance, outraged that I tried to keep her locked up all that time! As a result, I'd written lots more poetry and started two novels—one which did not take me very long to complete.

There were one or two more great bouts. One had started in 2013 and came creeping all the way into 2014. I penned lots of poems, quotes, short stories, essays, and have started three more big novels, a cookbook, and a memoir. No wonder my poor brain feels so exhausted much of the time!

Along with when I became so burned out on writing, I felt the same way about books as a source of reading. My brain was officially on strike, and I didn't even want to *read* anything. And when I did have to choke down some literature, I tried to do it as quickly as possible. The good thing was that I started to exercise a little more but, unfortunately, that did not last very long when I came back into writing.

In summation, let me just say one thing; I've come to the conclusion that I *cannot* quit writing, it's in my blood! This could be worse than many other addictions that I could have, so I may as well just stick to it.

12/20/14

One faithful day, the girl who was known as Jen Selinsky went insane. Nothing that was too irrational was the case, but she became overwhelmed from too much work. This work wasn't exactly difficult. It wasn't exactly emphasized, but this work was simply stressful.

As many very well may know, Jen was an anti-conformist, she wanted not to be drawn into society's realms. It seemed to her that all one had to do was know how to be conniving and manipulate. Is that all this world is coming to? What happened to obscure knowledge? It wouldn't be obscure if it were commonly used, now would it? It's a terrible idea to be tyrants to each other. She hates that— and especially having others tell her what they think she wants. No other mortal should be able to determine all that!

Crazy, I was crazy once. Mark Twain had a daughter that was once committed. The other two died, perhaps they were lucky in a sense.

Who wants to live that kind of life? Yet, I find we live it every day. Insanity becomes the pressure society tries to force on us, as we fit in and restrict our true feelings with age. Bah! What nonsense. Youth should be timeless!

1996 + 2008

Graduate School Application Letter

My name is Jenny Lynne Selinsky, and I was born in Magee Women's Hospital on November 2nd, 1978 in Pittsburgh, Pennsylvania.

My elementary school education took place at Haine Elementary School in Cranberry Township, Pennsylvania.

I then continued on to Seneca Valley Junior High and Seneca Valley High School, from which I graduated in 1997.

The fall semester of that year, I began my studies at Butler County Community College and majored in humanities. I earned my associate's degree in humanities in May of 2000.

I then started my education at Clarion University of Pennsylvania in the fall semester of 2000. I will be receiving my bachelor's in English in May of 2003.

In the year 1987, I joined the Brownies.

A few years later I became a Girl Scout and stayed in the troop until the end of the summer of 1991. We did a lot of activities, many of which included community service. I earned several badges for my efforts and achievements.

I made the honor roll in the first semester of my ninth grade year at Seneca Valley Junior High School. I've been on the dean's list four times so far in my college career. The first two times were at Butler County Community College in the fall of 1997 and the fall of 1999, earning a 4.0 grade point average both semesters. The other two times were at Clarion University in the fall semester of 2001 and the fall semester of 2002.

The extracurricular activities I've been involved in during high school include Art Club, Daily Poets Society, Bible Study, Girls Chorus, (which won medals for outstanding performance at Edinboro in 1996) and the Library Literary Club, of which I was Vice President my senior year.

As a student at Butler County Community College, I joined the Butler community choir called the Blazing Star. Our rehearsals took place in St. Paul's cathedral in Butler. We sang with the Butler symphony for their Christmas concert in 1998.

In the fall of 2001, I joined the English Club at Clarion University. I also joined the English Club honors fraternity, Sigma Tau Delta, in the fall of semester of 2002. During the same semester, I was also eligible to join Phi Sigma Pi, a National Honors Fraternity.

Some of my hobbies include reading, writing, and art. Over the years, my writings have been published in various newspapers and anthologies, one of them being Clarion University's literary magazine *Tobeco*. My latest accomplishments are my two books of poetry, *Opening the Doors*, (2001) and *A View of Dreams* (2002) which have been published through the online company www.greatunpublished.com. My illustrations are featured on the front covers. The complete number of poems I've written consists of over 4,000 in twenty-three books. At the present time, I am working on my first book of short stories.

I enjoy volunteering for different organizations. One of the groups I've volunteered for is called T.R.Y., which stands for "Together for Retarded Youth." I worked at their summer camp. My duties included supervision of campers, helping them with games and crafts, and creating fun activities for them to do. I participated in these summer camps in June of 1996 and 1999. Both years, I was awarded a certificate of appreciation signed by the coordinator of the organization.

I also volunteered several times to help with a community college sponsored clean up in Cranberry Township while I attended Butler County Community College.

I feel that I am a very well-rounded individual with many interests and abilities.

--January, 2003

My Timekeeper

I take off my watch and hear the little hands ticking. It just now turned 1:05 p.m. These little hands intrigue me, but they scare me at the same time. I know that my life is diminishing, but I like to see the second hand fly past, nonetheless. The face of the watch is clear of my fingerprint smudges. I hear the ticking, but it does not annoy me; it only bothers me while I am trying to sleep at night. Just thinking of the ticking is a bit disturbing, but it is another thing that shows that the watch is still working. The ticks are so small—small enough to match the size of the watch. I pick it up and notice that the leather is still smooth, and the only hard places are where they're supposed to be. The contrast in the texture makes it an interesting contraption indeed. I pick up my watch and hold it to my nose, and there is a slight odor of sweat that came seeping out from my wrist. Other than that, I can detect no scent. I hold it to my lips and lick the leather straps—an odd experience indeed. I guess the leather tastes like it's supposed to, but I do not know that for sure. I also taste a little bit of the nickel, but nothing is detected on my tongue. I'll refrain from doing anything further.

1/20/03

Little Things I Notice

My little fan is running, but my room is silent. Other than that, the darkness is contrasting with the light, as it looks even darker outside. I sleep with the light on every night. I place my hands on the windowpane and feel the coldness, like death moving in closer. The silence is nice but mysterious at the same time. Usually my eyes are drooping, like two heavy shades ready to fall down, thus blocking a person's view. Today, I am wide-awake, but I'm not quite ready to start the day. Even though it's still dark outside, I can see no one walking the campus. I did see a car or two drive by because it's that time when people start to get ready for their workday. Nothing else happened because the silence is still prominent. I have a few hours left before class starts, but I don't think I can go back to sleep.

1/28/03

Literary Response 1

At 7:00 p.m., on Saturday the 15th of February, I attended an open mic night at Michelle's Café. I brought my best friend, and her younger sister along because they also wanted the opportunity to read some of their poetry in front of a crowd.

Another friend joined us later, but he was only there to observe the event because he did not bring any of his own material to read.

At first, I was surprised at how crowded the café was. Even though the weather outside was far from promising, the event yielded a big turnout. It took a while for us to find a seat because the room was literally packed with people.

I missed the announcer and part of the first act. A person was in the middle of his first song as soon as I found my seat. His name eludes me at the moment, but I remember that the songs he covered were excellent, and it made me feel as if I were at a live concert. Since the room was still full, it took me a while to adjust to my settings and get comfortable.

The announcer came up to announce the second performer, and she filled in time by playing the part of a stand-up comedian while the second act was getting his guitar ready. His first song was a cover song, and the second one was something original that he said he thought of not long ago. This second song was very humorous.

Soon after, the announcer came to the table, and I asked her if I could sign in. It took me a while to notice that she was there because I was in the middle of writing a poem which I wanted to recite to the crowd. It was a birthday poem for Andy Taylor, the guitarist for Duran Duran (my favorite band). I told her I was not ready to go and asked her if she would put my friend before me.

As soon as Heather got up to speak, I felt excited for her because she never had the opportunity to do so before.

The announcer said she would let us each read two poems.

When Heather was nearing the end of her second poem, I felt the nervous feeling sink in.

As much as I love writing poetry, I know I am not very good at public speaking. That has never been one of my strongest areas. I was glad that Heather got this opportunity to speak, and it seemed like the audience really liked her work.

I got up to the microphone and had a seat on the stool. I knew most of the crowd had their eyes on me, but I maintained my cool. The first poem I read was from my second book, and it was basically a piece against the aging process.

After the first few lines of the poem, I felt more comfortable with the audience, and I knew that I had nothing to worry about. I delivered my second poem, about Andy, with ease. By that time, I had enough confidence to know that the audience was actually listening to my words. The applause I received at the end was rewarding, yet I was relieved to get back into my comfortable seat.

The two acts following mine were more musical acts. I cannot remember the names of the young ladies who performed, but they were both spectacular, especially the latter of the two. As I was sitting in my seat, listening to them play, I wondered if they ever seriously thought about sending their work to a record company. This added even more to my "concert experience."

I was a bit upset that the event only lasted for an hour, but I was glad I had this opportunity. This was a fun event to attend on a snowy Saturday night.

2/19/03

Literary Response 2

At 7:30 p.m., on Friday the 21st of March, I attended an open mic night at Michelle's Café. I was particularly excited about attending this event because Jan Beatty was the featured poet for the evening. All the other open mic nights I've attended in the past did not include a visiting writer, as they featured only students and faculty.

With me, as well as last time, was my best friend, Heather. She read three of her original works first, and I read three poems as well; two of which were mine, with one by Simon LeBon in between.

We arrived almost an hour early as to avoid the heavy crowd but, to our surprise, we were the first non-employees who entered the building at the time.

To pass the time, we talked to each other and started writing new poems. I noticed that a lot of the other people started coming in between 7:00 and 7:15 p.m.

Patrick Hicks was the announcer. After he officially opened the event, he read one of his pomes to start things off. I thought it was a good way to enter into the program.

Since Heather was the first who signed up to read, I made sure to give her some encouragement. The poems she read to the audience were excellent, and she seemed less nervous this time, as she added some excitement in her voice.

After she finished reading her poems were finished, I went up to the microphone, and found that I had to scrunch down a little because it was not adjusted to my height. I randomly picked out the first poem from one of my unpublished books which I had brought from which to read.

I was going to read the one from the left page first, but I decided it was a little risqué, so I turned to the right side and read that one. It was a little longer than one of my usual, early poems.

Then, I read one of Simon's more famous works, "This Is How a Road Gets Made."

The third poem I read was another random piece from my second published book. I was a bit nervous this time but, then, I had to recall all the times in the past that I had read and went through the incident with no problems.

There were a few other poets who read their works before Jan Beatty "took the stage," so to speak, at 8:00 p.m.

It actually took me a while before I recognized Jan because it had been approximately seven years since I had last seen her. At that time, I was in high school, and I met her at a local Borders bookstore on a library literary club field trip.

When Jan got up to the microphone, there was an explosive applause, then I glanced at her, wondering if she remembered my face. The poems she read were excellent, but I did not recognize them because they were from her newest book *Boneshaker*, which I did not yet have a chance to read. Her reading ran a little over half an hour, then followed a brief intermission.

It was during that time when I went up to her and introduced her to Heather.

The two of them shook hands, and she read one or two of my friend's poems.

Jan said that my face looked familiar, and I told her where we had met before.

She seemed to remember that day. I then gave her an autographed copy of my book, and then she let me pick out one of hers for free! I took the newest one, *Boneshaker*, since I did not have $8.00 at the time, but I did pick up the first book, *Ravenous*, which was $3.00.

After the intermission, the student and faculty readings picked up. I thought it was really nice that Jan stayed for the whole event.

Soon after Jan's reading came two young gentlemen who played some songs on guitar. They were the only performers who played instruments.

I thought it was great how Jan inspired the first guitarist to write a poem. I was under the impression that he really felt strongly about the subject matter about which he read, which always makes for a great poem.

Some of the later poems were about the current war, and it made me realize how important this event was. We came together not only to read and perform our works, but we came together, as concerned Americans, who want to see an end to all this irrational violence. During one point in the program, Pat even announced a peace rally that was soon to take place on campus. I hope that the event has a large turnout.

The whole event lasted three hours, but it was worth every minute of it! One of the most touching things was when Sasha O'Connor's father came up to the microphone and read the first poem he claimed to ever have written. For me, that seemed like a revelation; the more writers in the world, the better.

I must say that absolutely everyone who participated in the event was excellent, which made this event one of the best Friday nights I've ever had on campus.

3/25/03

Photo Exercise

I am bringing a new life into this world and, frankly, I am a bit frightened. This will be the story of a new mother, who has so many upcoming challenges to face. Through the love and support of my family, I know that I can get through whatever challenges that I must face. My mother has given me some good advice over the years, and I'll try to raise my child, as she has raised me. As far as the sex of the infant, I do not care what it is, as long as it's healthy. I know that my boy will become a fine young man, or I know that my girl will be a spectacular woman. People have told me, and I am certain that I will do this as best as I can.

3/27/03

Citino Response

I thought that the majority of David Citino's works were interesting because they are not much like anything that I've encountered before.

It did not take me long to figure out that many of his poems, in *The News and Other Poems*, dealt with death and human sexuality. One of the poems that stuck out in my mind the most was a work called "The Land of Liars," before which he starts out with a statistic.

The poem, itself, starts talking about the aspect of lying, and throws in the comparison of Pinocchio.

A bit later on, the work segues back into the statistics by categorizing people and what they lie about. The most interesting thing about that is that I can relate to some of these lies from experience, both at having said them myself and having heard others say pretty much the same things.

Other poems I really liked included "Ode to Billie Dove," "Payday," "The Meeting," "Two Lessons from the Sky," and "Cell Phone." I can particularly identify with the fourth because it discusses one of the most recent tragic events in our history.

Most of the other works I liked as well, but some of the concepts were a bit foreign to me because I did not know or could not relate to some of the subject matter. I will, however, pay more attention to these works upon my second reading of the book so I can embark upon some elements that I failed to notice before.

All in all, I have to say that I enjoyed reading the works of David Citino, and I look forward to attending the workshop and the reading later on today.

3/13/03

Education

*Written from the perspective of someone living in poverty, finally having the opportunity to attend college at Clarion U., for free, from a benefactor.

This room is the most magnificent that I have ever seen because this is a room in which I shall be taught. These teachings I will carry for the rest of my life, as they will be worth it someday, when I can find employment. Most of the desks are organized in a neat row, and my classmates are wearing decent attire, clothes that I could never imagine owning myself. For the most part, they seem cheerful and eager, even though I can say that my enthusiasm outshines all of theirs. The windows and doors are large and magnificent. Growing up in Iraq, I never would have expected to have such an opportunity.

4/17/03 + 12/4/14

Sentence Paragraph Exercise

"This place better have alcohol, or else I'm going to hitchhike back to Texas."

A man was standing in the lobby of an Outback Steakhouse, waiting for a seat and chatting with his friend. His tone suggested that he was kidding, but he did have on a T-shirt advertising Budweiser, and his southern accent was thick.

His friend said something to him shortly after, but it sounded like he was a native of Ohio, or at least he was from the general area. They ended up waiting for five more minutes, until they got a seat.

The two of them were taken to a booth, at which they sat down immediately. He looked at the drink menu right away to find that they did serve Budweiser, but he figured that he would try Foster's instead, since the restaurant had an Australian theme.

His friend laughed and made some remark about him trying new things. The man looked at him and smiled back. *Yep,* he thought to himself. *It would have been a long ride back to Texas.*

4/17/03

Expulsion Exercise

No longer will I be able to look at these blue walls and sit in these chairs that recently seemed so uncomfortable. Never again will I see the chalk caked on the blackboards, and no longer will I hear the laughter and comments of my classmates. Before, I used to look at the clock and try to push the hands forward but, now I want time to flow backwards; now I want to savor every minute that I can. The dreaded circle that I used to hate never seemed rounder and more perfect. It is as though I don't mind having my desk face my classmates. During the winter, I hate how the blinds used to be open, all the way-exposing me to the mess outside. Now, I would give anything just to see them, every day, again.

4/17/03 + 12/4/14

Music Appreciation

Being at this particular performance made me feel as if I was a child again. When I was ten to twelve years younger, I visited the circus quite frequently. I remembered the clowns, the animals, and the high jinkx.

All the sounds of the circus echoed in my mind as I heard the instruments being played. The very idea of combining a ringmaster with an opera announcer and a clown with an usher is very comical, and it is nothing that one would commonly use in symphony performances.

The young cellist, Lauren Sparrow, was so spectacular in her performance of Edouard Lalo's music. I find it very interesting that one of her age can be so committed to music, or any other area of interest for that matter.

The other fact that I found fascinating was that Lauren only started to play in the fourth grade, and she's already giving performances for famous musicians, such as Yo Yo Ma! That's only seven years of playing the cello. It's so amazing how one can go so far in such a small amount of time. It would probably take me twice as long to learn to play the piano, let alone the cello.

Strauss's *Til Eulenspeigel* reminded me of when I was a child; I played a few pranks myself. The story within the music goes to show us all how Til Eulenspeigel's spirit is still alive and, no matter how bad or good one claims to be, there is always a little mischief in him or her. I especially enjoyed this piece because it had a comical element nestled in it and a moral to the story as well.

The very final piece was the most familiar because I've heard many of those circus marches as I was growing up. The young gymnasts added to the atmosphere as well because of their bright costumes and the wonderful performance.

Those girls also reminded me of when I was young. I never took gymnastics, but the youthful looks on their faces paid a toll to my memory.

My experience at the performance was wonderful because it gave me a chance to relax and recall my childhood. If given the opportunity, I would see the show again because I had such a wonderful time. I think that everyone should take time out to recall their childhood and share it with their children. Don't you?

1998

Butler Symphony

I really enjoyed getting to practice and perform for the Butler Symphony Holiday Concert. The performance was so much more enjoyable than those in which I participated in high school because the atmosphere of St. Paul's church is nicer, and the members of the choir are much friendlier.

The commute was definitely worth it. And, even though the rehearsals were an hour and a half, the time still passed quickly. It was certainly nice getting to sing for all that time. This kind of music I particularly love.

Unfortunately, I missed the first part of the performance because I was just arriving, but I was informed that it was wonderful. They are an excellent symphony, and I appreciate them even more because I got to perform with them onstage.

My favorite piece of the performance was "O Holy Night," in French. I didn't think I would do well with the French accent, but it seemed easier than I thought it would be. The music that the symphony performed was exceedingly beautiful for the song; it gave me such a wonderful feeling, especially at the end.

Another wonderful part of the performance was getting to see the audience members and the content looks on their faces. In fact, those who came to see me were in my range of vision and, even though I couldn't quite see the expression on their faces, I'm definitely sure they enjoyed their experience.

I had a great feeling of contentment because never in my life, have I performed for such an appreciative audience. It seems to me that most of the people at the high school concerts were just there to see a family member perform, but the audience at the symphony seemed to really enjoy themselves, regardless of whether or not they knew someone performing. I think that's wonderful.

I'm just really glad to say that I've been a part of this, and I hope to perform with the symphony again when I have more time. I want to thank you, Mr. Rasely, for informing me of this because, if I didn't know, I would have missed a great experience.

1998

#1

Humanity did not know what to think about all the fighting and things going on down on earth. Ever since the beginning of time, man had not been at peace and, whether through means of peace or destruction, they sought ways to improve the situation. The year was 2010, and everyone was all a panic, until those who had not been creatures of the earth showed up and made the situation more bearable. Instead of destroying mankind, and vaporizing the earth, they intervened and told everyone that they were both right and incorrect at the same time. It was then when people began putting down their weapons and thoughts of hostility and thought to themselves, *Maybe these other beings are right. Their superb intelligence has allowed them to monitor our situation so they could give us input and tell us how to lead better lives.* As for the mystery of what is to come in the afterlife, no one is really quite sure because everyone still has different opinions, but they have allowed themselves to let go of their hostility regarding such matters. Though the question still remains, we will not fear what's to come because our otherworldly friends have shown us the error of our ways.

1/22/08

Piss poor and nothing to suck on—I hate it when the drought gets in here and makes me lose feeling in my fingers. Fuck all of you fascists. I don't know what I am saying or doing because that's why! Grieve no more, friend, as the shimmering light comes down and takes away my soul. No longer needing. No! She still can't be in here, which I whistle to myself to sleep. Creep, this just goes to show how I can bounce and dance and dance and bounce, until I can go la la and get through with the whole damn thing, sex in an elevator. You got no rite, man. You got no reason left behind your voice. And I bang my hands on the piano keys like to da la da to to da Whee! The blind lady does not see the words you're forming or the shows that fill my eyes. Time for such fools to realize that the shoe is on the wrong foot! Certainly to tell as nothing goes on inside the tiny mind of the tiny man inside the hotel room. I'm not prepared for such impending doom because I've forgotten how to tie my shoe! Whoo! Back to those days, I think not, because people don't even care to show how they don't feel & get rotten in a different life for a different time. No thank you, please. How disgusting! People like you have no decency on how to work the world and give them four reasons not to gravel on the ground (I am sound!)

1/22/08

My Inspiration

Grandparents, to most grandchildren, play just as important a role as one's parents do. They are just as wonderful and loving as any family member. My grandfather, Daniel E. Clarke, is a truly caring man. He has emphasized a lot to me during my lifetime and has maintained a pleasant personality. My grandfather is a great inspiration, being that he has inspired me greatly.

Ever since I was a young child, he had tried endlessly to make me a cultured and refined person. I was probably only five years of age when he gave me a set of classical records for children, and I still to this day admit that I have never listened to them too much.

When I was twelve years old, my grandfather had given me a version of *Peter Pan* to read. I still had not developed that interest yet, so he had to "bribe" me with something that I was interested in at the time. That was a bag of candy.

A year later, I showed some of my artwork to my grandparents. I have progressed so much from that time, but they still appreciated the fact that I was interested in art. Some of my more recent drawings are presently in their care.

In my early and middle adolescent years, my interest had started to develop because my grandfather inspired me even more. I started collecting books and became interested in music. I used to sing a few songs to them that we performed for the school choir, and they enjoyed hearing my voice. My grandfather, especially, was pleased to know that my culture and interests were developing with age.

My grandfather is not only an inspiration to me intellectually, but has taught me terrific values as well. He has taught me honesty and morality. Those are important values that dwell within my family, and grandfather has emphasized my using them for all of my life. He is also always concerned about Christianity and my attending a church. He has strong moral values and wanted me to follow his example.

Grandfather was also a well-respected man in the community in which he lives. He was a realtor by profession and served as the president of the Maryland state board of realtors. I have a bookmark with his picture printed on it at home, located in one of my poetry books.

My grandfather is truly a special man, for he has lived an exemplary life. The only part that I regret the most is the fact that he lives in Silver Spring, Maryland, and I only get to visit them three or four times a year. He lives with my grandmother, Marjorie L. Clarke, in a plan called Burnt Mills Hills, near a town called Hillandale. I feel very lucky to have such a wonderful grandfather. He has been a true guidance and inspiration to me my whole life.

9/25/96

A DEVIOUS TRAP

I do, hereby, declare that I have a problem with procrastination for the majority of my assignments, and I vow for my life to try to improve. The whole concept of procrastination is terrible, even to consider, because the result is having nothing accomplished by this ongoing, vicious cycle.

I hold this truth to this day I still procrastinate during the most inappropriate times. One could say that I am too much of a perfectionist, but I get everything accomplished at the last fraction of the minute. If an essay is due a certain day, I would say that I most likely complete it the night before!

Many also comment about the fact that I do procrastinate and/or put off studying for tests, and they are absolutely right. I would, and do, admit that I do not care for tests at all, so I despise studying unless it is something for my leisure time.

One shouldn't veto studying altogether if his grade is in danger, and all homework should be completed right away so that I can be done within a timely manner. I know that I like to get inconveniences done as soon as they are assigned.

Whoever is receiving the contents of what I'm trying to express, either by reading or listening, is prone to get the message eventually. Many are probably thinking, in their minds, that they simply don't care about their schoolwork or tests, but what about life? Suppose one fails to pay his bills on time, what would happen? Even something as simple as doing the Christmas shopping cannot be easily done without getting it over with right away.

I want to also emphasize that strain and worry from procrastination can sometimes hold dire results. Just think of dying from a substance overdose as a result of too much stress. This may be thought of as an exaggeration, but it is a possible truth. The result of procrastination, in the long run, could even lead to a direct suicide attempt from all the stress and anxiety built up in a person.

I have a terrible problem with procrastination, and I have made a vow to improve. Some good advice to my audience would be to diminish their procrastination levels as much as possible. It may not seem too relevant to many at the time, but please take my advice into consideration. The decision to procrastinate could be costly, as a result of a devious trap.

10/2/96

True Inspiration

A person, who was truly inspirational to me two years ago, is my tenth grade world literature teacher, Miss Schaudt, who has built on my literary view. She is presently in the intermediate building of the high school so, sometime, I should go visit her. I have been reading and writing ten times more since I've had Miss Schaudt as a teacher.

As some may very well know, I somewhat despised reading when I was a child. In my early adolescent years, I started to develop some interest in literature, but some other "environments" tended to rule the majority of my life. I was interested in things that many others of my age tended to gear toward. For quite some time, I watched the most absurd programs on television and tended to want to fit into society. I was falling into the trap.

My sophomore year with Miss Schaudt invoked a greater interest and emphasis in the arts. I became more cultured and versatile but, to the contrary, I became more practical. That was especially when we studied realism.

Not only did we study realism, but some international literature as well. We read some Asian myths and African ones. I had introductions to Petrarchan sonnets and Miguel De Cervantes's *Don Quioxte*. I now write stories based on some of these pieces of literature. Never much before have I written a derivative!

Still, to this day, I owe much credit to Miss Schaudt for all of the inspiration, which she has begun to give me, to create the pieces of literature that I do so now. I hope, for the future, that I continue to be inspired in writing as much as material as possible. I give true thanks to a terrific teacher!

11/17/96

Jim Morrison

Jim Morrison has been a true idol of mine for these past two years. His music and poetry has truly given me inspiration throughout this time period, and it has raised my mood when I was depressed.

The Doors are presently my favorite musical group, but not just because of the brilliant instrumental accompaniment, it was roughly his emotional and lyrical genius. I often times find myself listening to their music when I am definitely stressed out and/or depressed. Morrison has that assuaging power that serves as a "stress reliever."

Not only do I find The Doors as a stress reliever, but some of the messages in their songs emphasize freedom and transcendentalism. The Doors of perception, break on through to the other side! Our society sometimes perceives Morrison as a burden.

Why be tied down? Can one not live happier without all of the pressures of the world inflicted upon us? I myself choose to compromise, but only for the sake of "survival." After all, true freedom comes from a willing choice. Morrison implies love and beauty in his brilliant use of symbolism. I like the fact that most of Jim's messages are not stated bluntly because he gets my creative side kicking.

Many say that Morrison was basically a good for nothing drug addict and alcoholic, but I believe that is far from the truth. Our society tends to categorize him improperly. Morrison was indeed a kind, gentle and sensitive person. True, he did do drugs, but he had a lot of good qualities as well. He had a terrific sense of humor and great respect with love for others. Jim was adored by many, including his fellow band mates, and people he never even had an opportunity to meet.

The cause of Morrison's death, in 1971, was assumingly alcohol (not drug) related.

Varieties of people have told me that Morrison hadn't even used many drugs at all.

In my opinion, it was very sad that way that Jim had died. Let this be a lesson to us all.

My idol, Morrison, has played a very important role in my life for the past two years with his songs and his words. He will certainly be missed by many who have shared their lives with him, for they are the carriers of his generation to keep alive the memory of the Lizard King.

10/24/96

A shopping mall is nothing but a place where many go to waste time and money. It appears to be a social gathering, where people "flock" together and wander aimlessly for hours. For the most part, I despise shopping and all the time it involves. Couples walk hand in hand, for what better place is there to hold hands than the mall? Many of the stores tend to have annoying advertisements that the eye cannot help but notice. I'm tired of hearing from my peers that it is the "cool" thing to do because it is quite the contrary. What is there to do? Can't people fraternize elsewhere? I'm appalled by the number of people who choose to sit outside and smoke. Many of them tend to toss their butts on the lawn, rather than in the ashtray. The general environment is usually loud. I find it hard to focus on anything. Music is blaring from stores that I never even knew existed.

4/21/97

Driving is a wonderful activity because it enables one to relax and enjoy the environment. What I love the most about it is watching the scenery by looking out the windshield. Even though I spend most of my time paying attention to where I am going, I still look, with awe, at the scenery. The music I select usually puts me in a positive frame of mind, as I tend to relate it to where I am going. Passengers make it more fun, because I have some people with whom I can converse. Most of the enjoyment of driving comes from passing through familiar areas. I love traveling to the same places that I've been before. Most relaxation, for me, comes from driving.

4/21/97

With blue eyes and shoulder-length brown hair, he had a beautiful face. Six feet of height looked even taller because of his thin body.

On his top half, he wore a poet's shirt that had ruffled sleeves and buttons down the chest, the other half usually contained hip-hugging leather pants that sprawled down his thin legs.

On his feet were black cowboy boots, which seemed to compliment the outfit. In his mind, he was very brilliant, for he was gifted in verse. In his mind, poetry formed that he transferred to his notebooks.

In the mind of this man dwelled beliefs of transcendentalism. Main inspirations included non-conformity and freedom, as he tested the bounds of reality. Sometimes, the man was pompous in manner.

By provoking his friends, and others, he tried to make them become better people, for he had mischievous aspirations.

Childish games he played to see what kind of reactions he would receive.

Many problems were present during the time of his life, which he tried to avoid by immersing himself in alcohol. Family members were shunned, as he tried to isolate himself from them. Some problems had just begun when his alcohol and drug consumption commenced.

*Jim Morrison

3/26/97

Due to my negligence to fully understand the humorous mind of my father, I simply ignore the fact that I can't and go on with my life.

Many who have met him would surely agree that he is witty and humorous, but that is only the beginning. Just because he is witty and humorous at times doesn't mean that I always comprehend, or understand, that humor. His brain produces such absurd thoughts that it is hard to comprehend whether he is serious most of the time, or just the opposite.

I often wonder if his obscene screams to our young neighbors are meaningful, or is it simply the fact that he is blowing off steam that didn't go to his head from the cigar that he smoked. Sometimes, those kids shot BB guns and smoked on our property, and my father yelled at them outside. He added some sort of joke with the verbal warnings, and the way dad dressed is the most hilarious part of all, for he wore boxer shorts and nothing else.

When my father and mother converse with each other, I usually stay out of the discussion. What could be more confusing than hearing my father call my mother silly names? The worst part is that I can't understand at all whether he loves her, or he's really provoked. The thing that surprises me is that dad never apologizes for these asinine names he calls her, and my mother takes them with a grain of salt. Anyone could call that love.

Maybe it won't be until I'm old and grey-haired that I will fully understand my father's humor but, at least, I do understand the fact that it is only humor, and nothing else.

4/16/97

The writing process consists of six steps that one should follow if he or she wants his or her document to be effective. All these steps are integrated to make a piece of writing effective. Without one of these, the piece would not be as great as it should.

The first process of writing is prewriting, which mainly consists of jotting down thoughts of free writing. It follows the process of brainstorming. Prewriting doesn't necessarily have to be grammatically correct and/or in the sentence form because it is only the first step in composing the document.

The second step is composing. Composing is getting together all the thoughts and ideas and putting into sentences. When one composes, the document should take shape. The most important thing one should do is pick a subject and stay with it. All those ideas and thoughts one jotted down should be centering on the subject of the document.

The third step is conferencing, which entails the sharing of the document(s) with peers, family, or friends. What one does when conferencing is getting the opinions of others so that he or she can better his or her document.

One who is giving the opinions should always include some praise and some constructive criticism. The praise should comment on something in the document that is good and can remain as it is. The constructive criticism should consist of comments concerning polish and expansion. Polish pertains to things such as grammar and structure, and expansion consists of something that should be added upon the for sake of bettering the document.

The fourth of the steps is revision. Revision entails going back to all the constructive criticism that people gave. Once going back to the criticism, one can either except the suggestions, reject them, or get a second opinion. Those are the only three things one can do with the suggestions given to revise the paper.

The fifth step is editing, and it pertains to the grammatical features. After revision, one should go back and correct all the errors in grammar so that the document and/or phrases are accurate.

And, finally, when the piece is finished, one should publish his or her document. Publishing does not necessarily have to consist of having works accepted into a book or magazine, but it entails sharing the work with classmates, friends, family, etc. If a work was not shared, then how would it get recognition for all the steps that it underwent in the rest of the process?

That is my representation of the writing process. As one can see, one step is just as important as another. And, without all six, the document will lose its value. Who would have thought that writing effectively would come in only six, small steps?

12/4/99

Have you ever had the feeling that you were going to die? Your heart is vigorously pumping, and you don't even know what to do to stop it. Time grows short, as you gasp for what you think is your last breath of air. Hyperventilation commences. You're both dizzy and nauseous at the same time, and you hope to God that your ending will be sweet.

These are just a few of the symptoms one has when he or she is having an anxiety attack. Under most circumstances, the person is not going to die, but she thinks she is. Anxiety attacks are primarily mental ailments, but they can be cured by a strong, positive mind, or they can be cured by some prescribed medication.

These attacks have been affecting me since the age of sixteen. I am now twenty-one. Even though doctors have said that the attacks diminish with age, that may not always be the case with every individual.

There are, in fact, different branches of anxiety disorders. The first kind I had in my adolescence, and they are the acute and inconsistent panic attacks. The symptoms of these mainly include hyperventilation, crying, and the fear of something irrational, usually the fear of death and insanity. The attacks, themselves, usually last twenty to thirty minutes, and they can happen more than once a day. However, as I previously mentioned, there is no consistency. For anyone who has these symptoms, it would be best advised if he or she goes to a therapist, or psychologist, to get help with the treatment.

The other sorts of attacks are most like collected, irrational fears that can occur for many hours up to days. These fears entail a few short attacks that may involve some hyperventilation and a few other symptoms. In this case, however, the thoughts are built up for however long. The irrational fears can be diminished with the use of medications such as Paxil, Xanax, and Zoloft. Also, a strong mind, which can tell oneself that these fears are highly irrational, can aid in the reduction of anxiety.

Other incidents of anxiety can also be related to depression and Obsessive-Compulsive Disorder. They sometimes coincide, but medications, such as Prozac, can help cure the disorders and anxiety.

These cases, indeed, are horrible and unbearable. But, along with the symptoms, I have included possible treatments and cures for the problem. Again, I'd like to urge anyone who is reading the paper, if they have any of these symptoms, to go get help. After all, a peaceful mind leads to a non-stressful life.

12/3/99

Literacy

The word "literacy," for me, has more than one meaning. Literacy is being able to read and write, but it also entails having a certain amount of experience in doing so. The more one has read, the more literate that person is. This fact does not have to do with age, for anyone could be well read by the time they reach their early adolescence, and a person could be illiterate for their entire life.

I'm going to give a broad overview of my life, from the time that I was three years old, until the present. In the overview, I'm going to discuss the times of my life that I think were (and are) important in determining my literacy. Perhaps my definition will become clearer after reading this document.

When I was a young child, probably about three or four years old, I would watch my mother write letters to friends and relatives. Though I wasn't the brightest child of my time, I knew that she was writing. I was well aware of the fact that people wrote, but I was still unable to interpret the characters on the paper.

When I looked at the contents of the paper, all I saw consisted of a bunch of scribbles. I had no idea how to write at the time, but I tried it anyway. I took a piece of paper and a pen and tried to emulate the "scribbles" I saw on the paper. The end results looked all right to me, but I knew that my "writing" did not match up with hers.

She then came over to me, smiled, and asked if I was writing her a letter. My mother knew very well that I couldn't write, but she pretended along with me to make me feel as if I was doing something pleasing to both of us.

Behind my playful smile, I was really frustrated. What was she doing that I couldn't? I portrayed a sense of wonder and a sense of jealousy both at the same time. I knew that my mother was expressing herself by writing because I saw that people could pick up her letters and understand what she was saying.

She seemed like the most brilliant person in the world to me. The fact that she was able to write, however, seemed to infuriate me even more because I felt I was the only person who was unable to express herself by writing. I was determined to find out how she did it!

I remember that I actually began to learn how to read when I was in the midst of my first grade year. I was six or seven at the time. Most children probably began the process at age three or four, but I was not dismayed at my late coming.

My mother and I were simply ecstatic that I was able to read sentences in books. I remember where we were. We were in the waiting room of either my doctor or dentist. I had a book by Dr. Seuss in my hands, and I was pronouncing (as best as I could) the words out loud. First, I finished a sentence, and then, I finished a page. I kept going until I was all the way through, and I let out cries of joy when I was finished. I think my mother was happier than I at the time.

Between the ages of nine and twelve, I had mastered the basics of grammar and sentence structure. I was, however, no authority on the subject, nor will I ever be, but I kept (and keep) progressing as the years go by. I wasn't too sure about this whole "reading thing." Now that I was fully able to read and write, people were expecting more and more out of me. It drove me to the point that I almost hated reading, and writing, for that matter, as well.

All I seemed to care about was when the next episode of the *Teenage Mutant Ninja Turtles* was going to air and what kind of toys were out on the market. It never occurred to me that picking up a book and reading it for FUN was any kind of leisure activity that I was interested in. I thought that people who did that were complete and total nerds who had nothing better to do with their time.

By the time I was fourteen, I had my first publication. It wasn't much; it was only a story I had written for the *Back to the Future* fan club newsletter. And, since I was obviously a member, I received a copy in the mail. I noticed that the editor had made some revisions, and I was a little upset at that. But, now, I look back at it and realize that the revisions were for the betterment of the story. I can now show it off to people and proudly say that I wrote it.

The next year, when I was fifteen, I started to experiment with poetry. It was just something I felt like trying because I studied poetry more in depth during my freshman year in high school. I wanted to express myself using more than spoken words. I wrote ten to twenty poems in the year 1994, and all of them are in one of my fourteen complete books.

I had also written a few short stories, but they were never published or included in any of my books. I began reading a few contemporary novels, such as romance novels, suspense thrillers, and murder mysteries. Some of the ideas for my stories were based on them.

I was sixteen years old in the tenth grade when my interest in reading and writing really took off. I started to become a fan of The Doors, and Jim Morrison's lyrics gave me a lot of inspiration. Even though I'm not a big fan of The Doors anymore, I still must attribute my interest to Morrison and Kreiger's lyrics. They really gave my inspiration a jump start, and I was able to finish off a book or two of poetry because of them.

My reading interest became broader, as I started to become interested in classical and etiological mythology. My poems were dated and collected in manila folders so that I could keep track of them more easily. At that time, my family members and peers began reading some of my works. They were pleased with the outcome of the content, and they encouraged me to keep writing, no matter what the criticism. I really began to like what I was doing, and I felt a great sense of accomplishment from every work that I completed.

My sophomore year in high school was the same year that my English teacher, Miss Schaudt, stopped my mother in the hall of the intermediate school. The students' parents were attending an open house that night. Miss Schaudt recognized my mother from our last name, and she told her that she thought I was a remarkable student who always gave her input about the assigned readings from class. The same teacher also sent me an application in the mail for some kind of student award for excellence in the classroom. I declined the application, however, because I feared I would not measure up and be rejected for the reward.

The next year, my junior year, I was more literary in the sense that I started getting into novels of the nineteenth century. I had a class in American literature, and it really influenced my thinking. One of my favorite writers at the time was Mark Twain. We read a variety of works in that class, and one of them was *The Adventures of Huckleberry Finn*.

I enjoyed the book so much that I read it twice in the same year, even though the second reading was not required for class. I was so intrigued by him that I wrote a fantastic paper concerning his life and some of his literary works. My homeroom teacher, unfortunately, threw it away during locker clean out at the end of the school year. I was absent that day and she cleaned out my locker for me! I even saw a production that summer, which was given by the family dermatologist. (I kid you not.) He was a big fan of the writer, and he took on his persona and performed some of his works. I'm glad that I didn't miss that opportunity!

Also, at the end of the academic year, I got published in our school's literary club booklet. I joined that year because I wanted to prove my love for literature, and I certainly don't regret my decision to do that. I was also involved with a group called The Daily Poet's Society, which entailed every member writing a poem every school day and posting them in manila folders. At the end of the year, they were supposed to be published, but the project fell through when the man in charge put in his retirement.

My senior year of high school consisted of three separate publications. One was in the school's literary journal, one was for a library anthology, and the other was for a poetry anthology. My interest in reading shifted over to writing. I was elected vice president of the Literary Club, and I finished my first complete poetry book in March of that year. We also had a poet, Samuel Hazo, come to visit the school. He is the author of many books in many literary genres. I also found that I wrote a poem similar to his, so I typed it out and gave him a copy, and it seemed that we were both impressed with each other's works.

I'm going to skip ahead until this past October. Emily Dickinson was noted for having written approximately 1,800 poems. I exceeded the goal I set for myself after reaching 2,000 poems, and, thereby, surpassing her volume of poetry written. I was just a few weeks shy of turning twenty-two, and I had written eleven complete books of poetry.

Currently, I'm a second semester student at the university, having transferred with my associate's degree in humanities from Butler County Community College. I have just finished writing my thirteenth book of poetry. My last count of my poems was approximately 2,220 poems.

All my books are unpublished, but I am currently working on changing that. In the twelfth and thirteenth book, I also have many poems attributed to my favorite rock group, Duran Duran. Their music has touched me in a mystical sense, and it has inspired me to write of more optimistic topics, such as sensuality and freedom. They do not, however, play as big a part as The Doors in providing me with overall inspiration.

I am very happy to say that I have a collection of books, autographs, and photographs of some of the writers who have visited the school this year: David Drayer, Robert Gibb, Ann Pancake, and Dennis Brutis. I even found a copy of Dr. Terman's poetry for sale at the university bookstore.

Their works are extremely impressive, and I had them all sign the fronts of some of my books. I am looking forward to later in the semester, when more writers will be visiting the university because it's very interesting to get to talk with them and find out what inspired them for their works.

For me, poetry is a wonderful form of self-expression, and I take great joy in spending more of my leisure time producing ideas and getting them on paper. That's probably why many people see me, as I do, as such a prolific writer. With written word, the emotions stay on the paper and can be immortalized, whereas spoken word disappears into the air as soon as everything is stated. It's much easier to extract ideas and meanings from written works in general.

The word "literacy" has a flexible meaning, and any person can determine what literacy is and how they are by themselves. The important thing to remember about literacy is that just knowing how to read and write is not enough.

One has to enjoy it and experience what's out in the world to get the full effect. I went from being a bewildered and frustrated three-year-old, who had no idea how to read or write to a twenty-two-year-old student, who does these activities on a daily basis for enjoyment.

Besides the literary biography I wrote about myself, my main point is to encourage others who read the document to become more literate themselves. Not only is literacy an important accomplishment, but it's a satisfying one as well.

2/2/01

Writing is one thing that I spend the majority of my time thinking about and trying to improve. I'd say that my history is a little plant and sprout and continuing to grow.

For the first few years of my life, I quite despised to write because my creativity was just starting to grow past a seedling. Writing was not quite interesting to me yet, so I usually expressed myself through artwork. The seed was commencing to erupt.

A year or two before junior high, one could notice a bit of green poking out of the seed in the dirt. I composed a few poems and short stories for mere school assignments, but subtly my interest started to develop.

Seventh grade through my freshman year, more green was showing. I began to write (at that time) a few short stories during my leisure hours. I was definitely improving, but I still didn't figure too much. Reading more books also helped improve my mind, being that it had boosted my creativity. In fact, I wanted to write even more! That also helped me to get a story published in a column of the *Back to the Future* fan club newsletter in the summer of 1993.

My sophomore year, look out! This little bud had started to grow higher out of the dirt! My reading interest wasn't as great as it is today, but I did love to write. I had (then) started rough drafts for books and novels. I must have started about two or three. Also, poetry became relevant in both my school work and leisure time! Nothing could stop me; I was a writing machine. Dozens of poems were produced during my sophomore year, and I still have them to this day (up in my room). I also started to read more as well.

Summer of 1995, I started purchasing more books. However, the stem remained practically the same. I don't remember writing too much during that time period (except some poetry), but my reading developed some time later.

The beginning of my junior year, my writing flourished as well as my reading. In study halls for both semesters, I composed more rough drafts of books. I wrote twice as much poetry for the school's Daily Poet's Society, (too bad it was never published). That stem was growing more and more!

I also liked to share my writing with the Library Literary Club. Later, at the end of eleventh grade, I had another publishing opportunity from the librarians to have some poetry collected in a small booklet. Three of my entries were included.

In the recent summer of 1996, most of my writing dealt with another small beginning of a manuscript, letters to friends, and birthday poems. The green was starting to develop into form. Both of my grandparents and great aunt had birthdays this summer. I wrote poems for them all, and I entered a poetry contest in Maryland. Some of my friends appreciated the letters, and actually wrote back! This summer was terrific!!

I am now a senior in high school, and this is my final year. I now realize that I must be more realistic and wise for the future. That stem may only grow to be that of a rose, or the size of the tree, with roots symbolizing the present. It could be said that I'll never know ahead of time what my literary future will hold, but I have extremely high hopes for the growing stem to continue its process.

8/31/96

My name is Jen Selinsky, and I was born in 1978 in Pittsburgh, Pennsylvania. I was raised in and lived most of my life in a growing suburb approximately twenty minutes north of Pittsburgh, called Cranberry Township.

In June of 1997, I graduated from Seneca Valley Senior High School.

In December of 2004, I received my MLS in Library Science from Clarion University of Pennsylvania, and I moved to Sellersburg in late February of 2005 as a result of me getting a job with the Charlestown-Clark County Public Library system.

I currently work as Head of Collection Development at the Sellersburg branch Library, and I have been there for nearly a year and a half.

When I was fourteen, I had my first publication, which was in a newsletter for a fan club. It involved a fictional story about characters from a movie. A year later, I also "reworked" William Shakespeare's *Romeo and Juliet* and sent it to the Walt Disney Company.

Even though my "manuscript" was declined, I thought it was nice that the company gave me a response, stating the reasons why the work was not accepted.

I have always had a vivid imagination, but my real love for writing began around the time when I was fifteen. During the summer of 1994, I started writing poems, and I continued slowly, but surely until the start of my junior year in high school, when I started writing more for an after school group called The Daily Poet's Society. We were supposed to have our woks published in a student anthology at the end of the school year, but the person in charge retired, and none of the poems got published at the time.

Later that year, another club with which I was involved, the Library Literary Club, had some of its members write poems and short stories, which were "published" in a small booklet and given to the students soon before school let out.

Once I began my senior year, I got published in a book of poetry anthologies. I was very excited since this was my "first real publication." Also, the public libraries affiliated with my high school initiated a contest for the students from kindergarten to twelfth grade.

Even though I did not win any of the prizes, one of my poems was published in the collection. I also had another poem and one short prose work published in our high school literary journal, *The Raider Review*.

In June of 2001, I had my first books of poems published by a small online company, which was known as www.greatunpublished.com. The title of the book is *Opening the Doors*, and it was a compilation of what were thought of as my best poems from my first fourteen books.

The following year, I another title published under the same company. *A View of Dreams* was my first book of actual poems that I wrote. Since then, the company has become known as Booksurge, www.booksurge.com, and was recently purchased by Amazon. My first two titles can be found and purchased by author or title at most any online bookstore, including,

www.amazon.com , www.barnesandnoble.com, and www.borders.com.

From 2003 to 2005, I started writing more poems, thus adding to my collection.

In 2002, I managed to get one of my poems published in the literary magazine for Clarion University, *Tobeco*. It had been a few years since I published anything on Booksurge, and most of my works were not ready for publication.

Last August, one of my best friends told me about a site called www.lulu.com that published books and other materials from FREE. Authors can set their own prices for royalties, and the company includes copyright options for all materials. Those who are members also have the option of purchasing an ISBN for nationwide or worldwide distribution.

If you are interested in learning more about Lulu, you can log onto their website.

Ever since last September, I have been publishing books there, and I currently have thirteen titles on Lulu available for purchase. I will be handing out my business cards attached with a recent article about www.lulu.com from the June 12th *Courier Journal*.

Up to date, I have written fifty books of poetry. As soon as I finish my fifty first, I am going to "retire" from writing poetry so I can get caught up on publishing my completed books and develop my prose skills.

Though I am primarily known for my poetry, I have completed one children's book, and I am currently working on five prose titles. I am also looking to expand my horizons from Lulu and Booksurge to other publishing companies. My goal is to become a diverse writer with published books in many different genres. Thank you all for your interest in my works.

6/21/06

Writing, for me, is the one thing that I spend the majority of my time thinking about and doing. And, day by day, I am trying to improve my skills. I'd say that my writing history is just a little bit past a small tree, and it's continuing to grow. I hope to keep writing for the rest of my life. I want my writing skills to grow, as a strong oak tree grows from a young seedling.

During the first few years of my life, I despised writing because I lacked the creativity; it was just starting to grow past that of a seedling. I held no interest for writing whatsoever, and I mainly expressed myself through artwork. I have always loved to draw and paint. Art is really enjoyable, and it's a good way to express myself creatively. My thoughts and ideas are important and expressed throughout my art. The seeding was commencing to erupt.

A year or two before junior high, one could notice a bit of green poking out of the seed in the dirt. I composed a few pieces of prose for school assignments for, subtly, my interest started to develop. I realized while doing these assignments, that I enjoyed the process and my growth continued.

Seventh grade through my freshman year, more green was springing forth, I composed a few short stories during my leisure time. I was definitely improving, but I didn't figure too much. Reading more books also helped my creativity, and it enhanced my vocabulary, thus improving my writing abilities. It was during this time that I actually began to enjoy writing as a leisure activity. That actually helped me to get a story published in a column of the *Back to the Future* fan club newsletter in 1993. I was proud of this accomplishment and felt a desire to have more work published.

My sophomore year, look out! The little bud had started to grow higher out of the dirt! My reading interest wasn't as great as it is today, but I did thoroughly enjoy writing. I had even started rough drafts for stage performances and novels.

Poetry became the most prevalent form of my writing and the thing I enjoyed the most for schoolwork and my leisure time.

Nothing could have stopped me because I was a writing machine! Dozens of poems were produced during my tenth grade year, and, to this day, I have well over 1,400 poems.

During the summer of 1995, I started to purchase more books. However, the stem remained practically the same. I don't recall having written too much prose during the time, but my reading had certainly developed.

The beginning of my junior year, my reading and my writing had flourished, as I became more prolific. In study halls for both semesters, I composed more rough drafts for books.

I wrote twice as many poems for the high school's Daily Poet Society (which, unfortunately, never became published). The stem was growing more by the day. Soon it would grow stronger. As the oak flourished, so did my writing.

I also liked to share my writing with the school's Library Literary Club. And, during the end of my junior year, I had another opportunity to become published.

The main librarians collected writings from the students in the Literary Club, and they put them together in a book of compilations. Three of my entries were included.

During the later part of 1996, I wrote letters to many friends and family members, and I included some of my poetry in a few. I entered a poetry contest in Maryland and got my third publication in another book of compilations. The stem had grown a few more inches high and became wider, broader, and straighter.

By the time I reached my freshman year in college, the trunk began to multiply and grow leaves. I was determined to get some works published in the 1998 edition of *Facets*, but I was never informed, either way, if my works were accepted. However, I was writing a lot of prose for homework assignments in my classes for both semesters, and my poetry was starting to transfer from loose-leaf paper to personal, hardback journals.

My sophomore year in college involved taking the 800 or so poems that I had written and putting them into the hardback journals. By that time, I had four books completed, and I hadn't planned on stopping. The leaves attached to the large trunk spread all over the place.

I am now a junior at BCCC, and I plan to graduate with an associate's degree in humanities this spring. I have seven books of poetry completed, and I am currently

working on my eighth and ninth. For many years of my
life, writing has been so important to me, and I hope that
the small tree which exists today grows to be full and
healthy in the years to come.

1999

I live in the United States, on the east coast, in western Pennsylvania. My current residence is at Clarion University. I aim to obtain good grades and get my bachelor's degree in English.

My life is relatively simple; I look forward to many things, but I take one day at a time. I feel that I have no great purpose in this life but to make people happy with themselves. Sometimes, I put my priorities behind those of others so that they will be pleased. Some people say that I like to take in society's misfits and give them the love that they never had.

Others say that I am a martyr of sorts; I suffer when others are showing their grief. My happiness highly depends on that of my friends and family.

Those who are closest to me say that my existence is dull; they think that I need to take more advantage of daily events. I'm not too fond of the idea of physical labor, and several of my loved ones are trying to push me to work more.

I like to take things easy and take every opportunity that I can to relax. I'm very much a loner, but I am sociable in familiar company. But this is what I live for,

loving others and having time alone makes me happy. I
have love for others and myself.

9/18/01

John Haines Response Paper

Last Thursday evening, I had the distinct privilege of meeting John Haines, poet and artist. The reading took place at 7:30 p.m. in Moore Hall.

Haines is a delightful man who was not afraid to tell us of the things that he encountered. Despite all of the prestige he has gained over the years, I was very surprised to find that he was a modest man.

Haines has published fourteen books in his lifetime, and the works included within are spectacular. A few of my favorites include "The Whale in the Blue Washing Machine," "Green Piano," and "Life in an Ashtray." The latter of the three I found to be the most compelling. It describes the horrors of smoking and the tobacco industry.

John Haines has lived an extraordinary life, and one could safely assume that some of his major influences are Emerson and Thoreau. He was a self-made man, who has lived in the state of Alaska for twenty-five years. Haines lived a simple life and (presumedly) gave up many modern conveniences for carrying out his deeds. Before he took writing seriously, Haines attended college to major in visual arts.

The writer even told me, himself, that he has heard others, such as Robert Frost deliver their works into the public.

Frost was "notorious" for not being a good reader in public. Just the opposite was true for John Haines. He went up to the podium with the kind of confidence that some speakers lack. The delivery of his words was beautiful, and I could tell that the whole audience (including myself) was intrigued by his ease of speaking.

The most exciting part of the evening was getting to go out to dinner with John Haines, the faculty, and the students. The writer recited a funny poem that parodied Robert Frost's "Stopping by the Woods on a Snowy Evening." It was such a personal experience. John Haines is an excellent writer, and I'm glad that I got the opportunity to meet him. It's a memory that will last a lifetime!

9/25/01

Oppression Paragraph

In February of 1994, I was at the local Sheraton Inn. I had a membership for the pool, and I showed up quite frequently. Not many people were present, so I had most of the area to myself. Four boys, about sixteen or seventeen years old, noticed me when I went into the pool. Within a matter of seconds, they all crowded around me. At first, the attention was flattering, but I grew more and more uncomfortable as time went by. They wanted to be alone with me, but I refused. Despite their disappointment, they did not relent. I felt oppressed because of the sexism that was present; they gave me the impression that they only wanted one thing. It finally took the lifeguard to come over and tell them to leave me alone. Not many people would feel the same as me, but I felt oppressed because of the sexism that occurred. I'm glad that I was able to escape a dangerous situation, and I'm also glad that someone else was looking out for my welfare.

10/9/01

The Reading

Eamon Grennan is an Irish poet, originally from Dublin. He's been living in the United States for several years, and he is currently a teacher's assistant at a university in the state of California. Grennan said that he is not the type to go around looking for inspiration. Rather, he lets inspiration find him.

At the 7:00 p.m. reading in Hart Chapel, he read approximately sixteen poems from one of his books. The first few poems dealt with the concept of art, some of which expressed using violence as a medium. The rest, and the majority of his works, involved reminiscing about times past.

The fourth poem he read, "Porridge," talked about how, when he was a child, he remembered the smells of his kitchen and the surrounding areas. The poem was so effective in its composition and deliverance that it got me to identify with the subject by having me actually think that I was in the same setting.

Three of the most touching poems that Grennan read to us were those involving his children. He had written a splendid poem for each of them. The two poems about his daughters dealt with their beauty and their skills, and, therefore, were very touching in their nature. Whereas, the poem about his son described a streaking incident he and his friends took part in after finishing final examinations. It seems that Grennan is a compassionate man with a lot of love for his children, and one can truly see that in his excellent works of poetry.

After he read three more of his poems, the reading came to an end. I was surprised to find that Grennan did not further discuss his works after they were read. He simply said a few words and walked off the stage.

The audience gave a warm applause to show their satisfaction with the performance. Eamon Grennan did a wonderful job, and I won't be surprised if he's asked to come visit the university for a third time.

Previously in the year, I had seen the other visiting writers, David Drayer, Robert Gibb, Ann Pancake, Dennis Brutis, and Lee Gutkind, but none of their works touched me as Eamon Grennan's did. I believe that he is the best writer that I've witnessed so far, and I look forward to a possible visit from him, on campus, sometime in the future.

3/13/01

Ed Jensen is seventeen years old and has quite a "unique" personality for his age. He has a fun-loving, but worrisome personality that is sometimes frowned upon by his father. His shoulder-length golden hair never tends to get in the way of or cover his semi-pale face because it is always pushed to the back of his head. Ed has turquoise blue eyes that don't seem to match the rest of him at all, so they are sometimes questioned by his inquisitive peers. His skin matches that of his face, with the partly tanned flesh he has had most of his life. Ed's large goldenrod eyebrows, that match his hair, sit in a position at the bottom of his forehead. His build is similar to that of an "average" young male's. He has plenty of strength that is basically divided equally amongst him, and weighs approximately 175 lbs. His clothing attire mainly consists of flannel shirts, faded jeans, and brown hiking boots. Ed has traits and characteristics that make him unique from others.

9/5/96

The Object of Focus

A pinewood paintbrush is on the floor of my bedroom as I lie on the floor and stare at it. I notice the finish on the grip of the brush, as it is still perfectly glossed over, but the brush is not flawless. Small amounts of color are seen at the bottom of the brush. Orange, yellow, and red. I realize that I have not cleaned it out thoroughly.

The small bristles of the brush are not welded together because of wetness, but they are separate and disorganized from being dry. They feel like matted pieces of fur that was torn off that of any mammal's back and given to me. A small mass of a whole collaboration of little bristles are sticking out in all directions. I try to fuse them back together, but gravity will have its way in keeping them separate.

No distinct odor of turpentine is detected from this paintbrush being that I haven't used it for quite some time. It just lie there, motionless.

I then decide that I am tired of looking at the paintbrush, so I pick it up. The size of it is relatively large, but not too much bigger than any of my others. I feel the smoothness in my hand, as it almost falls down unto the floor. Then, I neatly put it back into my closet, with all of the other paintbrushes that look much worse than that one.

10/28/96

Experience Paper

Dr. Philip Terman is an English professor at Clarion University, who teaches in Davis Hall. Several years ago, he started a program called the Spoken Arts Series, in which various visiting writers come to the university and talk about and read their works. Faculty members, such as Dr. Herbert Luthin, have read their works in the past, but on the evening of September 23, 2004, Dr. Terman read his works from his second and newly published book of poetry, *Book of the Unbroken Days*.

Since I am one of the new hosts/anchors for the university television show, *Literary Lust*, I felt that my attendance at the reading would be beneficial, since I will be doing commentary on the show.

Dr. Terman, through his inspirational poems, talked about his culture and his life experience. Most of his works had to do with the changing of seasons—summer into fall in particular. His beautiful use of imagery brings his works to life as they are read from the pages.

The evening was rich with multiculturalism, as Dr. Terman also talked about his origin and religious background. Since he is of Jewish heritage, some of the works he read had to do with questions of life, concerning his religion and experiences, that ran through his mind while present in the. He has two adopted daughters from China, and he mentions aspects of their native culture as well. The last poem he read was the longest, and it was the self-titled work from the book *Book of the Unbroken Days*. Dr. Terman said that his inspiration came from a portion of the Book of Isaiah, as its themes are reflected in the work.

Dr. Terman read his works in such a way that an audience would be able to relate. His captivating imagery opens up the imaginations of his audience and gets them to think on another level. I especially liked his religious questions and reflections on life because I find myself pondering similar things. This was certainly a wonderful experience, and I am glad to have been a part of the audience for this reading.

9/30/04

Homework: 1-3 pages on fears, worries, and expectations

Before I got here, I thought all the teachers would be pains. But, after the first day, they were all rad. I also thought I couldn't open the locker either but, today, I found out how. I also like stuff about this school. You don't have to stay here all day because you get home earlier than elementary. You also change classes too so you won't be in the same room all day. But I hate it more than anything when there is hardly any room to walk around in the halls. And when you can't find the class you're in next and the bell rings. All the classes are rad so far. The schedule was wrecked because the computer messed it up. I also expect there will be lots of tests! Mr. Shaw, Miss Apple, and Mrs. Stewart are my favorite teachers so far. But I also like Mrs. Snyder, my study hall teachers, and Mrs. Booker. I didn't meet my gym, art, French, Spanish, and reading teacher yet.

I like Study Hall because it gives you time to do your work. I also like science because we are gonna do interesting things. I think I'm also going to like language, too, because it's interesting, and the extra points give you a chance to help your grade. My sister said my gym teacher is an awesome dudette. But she doesn't know half of my teachers because they're new, but I like the school itself. If I study real hard, I will get the best grades. There is another thing I hate about school. It's only the 2nd day of September, and I have to go to bed early! At least I can open the locker now, but I still have trouble finding the rooms. I think this year will be exciting. When I get home, I do my homework that I didn't finish at study hall.

I also like school because you don't have speakers that announce busses. They're all parked in front of the school. My reading teacher's name is Mrs. Brewer. She is a very nice teacher. She is in Mod B. She said she read fifteen books over the summer. Reading is my last period. Our bus ride is thirty minutes long. We have to wear a gym uniform. We have Mr. Shaw for music.

-1991

I don't think my parents push me to do anything because, when they ask me to do anything, I do it gladly. When I get home, I do my homework, then I help them.

I go to bed every nite at 10:00, and I wake up at 6:15 if it isn't Saturday or Sunday. And, on weekends, I help my parents with the laundry. Also, on Halloween, I help my parents with the candy.

If I have a test, I go in my room and study for one hour then have a break if it's anything but a spelling test. Sometimes, I clean my parents' room and make up their bed. In the fall, I help dad rake the leaves, but we never finish the whole backyard. But I never helped mow the lawn. My parents don't push me.

10/30/91

In this class so far, I learned about diagramming parts of speech. I like when we learn about parts of speech. We have a little too much homework. I hate the idea that we have to make the diagrams absolutely perfect, or it's wrong. I liked the first day essay. I didn't really like the book report. But it wasn't my least favorite thing to do in the class. I don't want to be mean, but I wish we could have more fun. I don't have a worst thing we did yet. I like the idea of the grading chart, where we keep all of our grades.

I also like one more *important* detail. The teacher. You're one of my favorite teachers. Don't give me an A just because I wrote that. I really meant what I wrote. Anyway, that was a good idea about using a three-ring notebook, and I think the name thing we made was cool, even though I had to use my last name.

That was interesting about the difference between nouns and pronouns. I like English.

1991

I like spring because it's way better than winter, no cold or anything. That also means it will be warmer outside, and school is almost out. Some of the signs are that it's getting warmer and snow's starting to melt. I change when spring comes. Then I'm in a better mood, and I go outside more. All of the seasons change my mood. In fall, I'm, like, OK. In winter, I'm in a bad mood a lot. In spring, I'm in a better mood. In summer, I'm like, "Yes, school's over."

We had a couple nice days in February. But spring will be much better. It also rains a lot in the spring because that's when all of the flowers and animals are born. Spring is like a lovely season. All kinds of life is born. Much better than winter. I *hate* spring cleaning.

1992

This summer, I'm going to do a lot of things. This summer, starting June 7th, I start youth group every Sunday. And, starting June 9th, I have art class every Tuesday.

I'm also going to sign up for two pools—one's indoors, and one's outdoors. Maybe, if we're lucky, we'll go to North Carolina.

My friend and I are also going to Kennywood. Those are all of the main events of the summer, except for maybe going to our grandparents.

I also have a week-long summer camp and a week-long intermediate swim lessons. My friend also has a swimming pool in her backyard. I could also swim there.

There are also days that will be crappy, slow, and boring. If that happens, I would read a book, watch TV, and watch my favorite movie, *Back to the Future*. I'll watch that, anyway.

If it is a nice day, I could go outside and ride my bike or go over my friend's house. I look forward to weekends because I can sleep in Saturday and Sunday.

I can also stay up after 10:00 on Friday and Saturday night. But when summer comes, I can stay up every night and sleep in every day unless, of course, I have to go to church or something. I'm also looking forward to not have to do any more school or homework. That will be fun.

Summer is my favorite time of the year because the weather is nice, and there's no more school work of any kind to do. And when summer's here, that means spring's over and no more spring cleaning.

I really can't write much more because I already wrote all of the things I'll do this summer.

1992

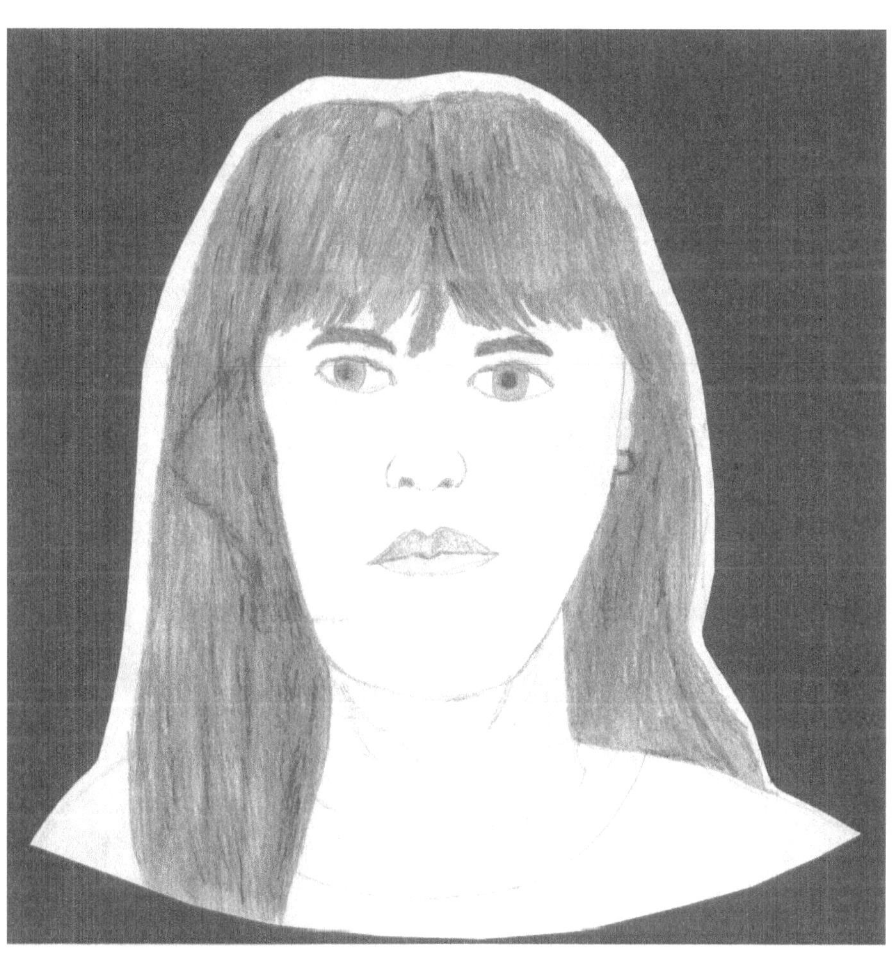

2003

Caption for Power Portrait

I am an individual who dares to dream and wants to be taken seriously. Over the last few years, I have dedicated my life to my studies, and I strive to better myself through the use of my talents and my intellect. Though some of my thoughts may be extreme, and some of my ideas may be abstract, I like to challenge others to understand the depths of me. I will not be deterred by the remarks made by those who only wish to damage my willpower and my state of being. Someday, I hope that people will be able to look back on my life and know that I have accomplished a lot because I want to be known as a person who has done something great with her time.

4/4/03

The reason why I dislike television talk shows is because their topics seem so fake and ridiculous. It seems like they're always going for high ratings by choosing sensationalized topics. The shows seem to be addicting, as my mother is "hooked" on the famous favorites. She tapes them at day and watches them at night.

I don't watch them, but I'll walk through the room occasionally when one of them in on. I just can't believe some of the junk they have on. The only interesting thing about them is to watch some of them lose, gain, and re-lose weight over the years!

But, apparently, some people like them since they've been on the air for quite a number of years.

6/2/94

One of my most embarrassing moments happened about three years ago. I was at Kennywood Park with my friend and my mother. I had brought an extra set of clothes to change into after I went on the Raging Rapids. I forgot to bring an extra bra. So, I turned to take off my sweatshirt, but the T-shirt stuck to it, and I ended up flashing the people in front of me.

My friend didn't see it, but my mom did. She was horrified; she just wanted to disappear. I was also really embarrassed, too!

I subscribe to a magazine called *YM*, and they have a column called Say Anything. It's about people's embarrassing moments, so I submitted this incident to them, but they did not print it. I guess this seems "tame" compared to some of the other stories.

6/2/94

I want to tell you about my best friend. Her name is Jen Stockett, and I've known her for about 1 and ½ years. She was in my gym class last year, and I started talking to her. Back then, she was so shy but, through the months, I got her out of her shell. Now, mostly, she calls me, and she's the one who starts the conversations.

I'm really glad I have her as a friend because we do a lot together. We go for walks in Harmony, (where she lives), we go swimming together, and we see movies together.

We're both also in chorus together. (She's a 1st alto, and I'm a 1st soprano.) We both also really enjoy singing.

I'm glad to have her as my best friend, and I hope we'll be friends forever.

6/2/94

One of my favorite singers is Mariah Carey. My mother has a friend named Margie, whose brother-in-law is the Vice President of Sony Records. He works directly under Tommy Mattola, who's president of Sony Records and also Mariah Carey's husband.

When they got married last September, her brother-in-law was invited to the wedding in New York. The wedding was a lavish affair with lots of celebrities and rich people.

They weren't able to go the wedding because they couldn't think of a gift over $1,000 dollars.

I don't know Margie, or her brother-in-law, personally, but I would like to meet them sometime. Hopefully, I will also get to meet Tom and Mariah someday. Who knows, maybe I'll get to go one of her concerts free someday!

6/2/94

I really don't remember too much about my childhood, but I'll try the best I can. I remember about three or four years ago, I was basically the opposite of what I am now. I was playful, happy-go-lucky, and wild. I had a favorite cartoon that I used to like, (which I'm quite embarrassed of mentioning). It was *Teenage Mutant Ninja Turtles*! I used to love that show more than anything. I also really wasn't boy crazy yet, I didn't care for guys! I also hated music!

One main thing was that I hated talk about relationships (boyfriend + girlfriend) and serious issues. I always thought my life was worse back then but, as of now, I feel like it was better!

12/10/03

I have a lot to do this Christmas. First, I have to go to Maryland to see my grandparents. (That's probably the only place I'm going!) Even though I don't really want to go, that'll be Christmas Day!

Then a day or two after Christmas, my dad's parents from Philly are driving to our house to celebrate Christmas (a day or two late). They're staying over our house two nights. Then they'll go back home.

Last, but not least, New Year's Eve, I'm going to my friend's house to sleep over. (Sleep may not be the word. Knowing us, we'll be up all night, or at least 'til twelve)! Who knows, maybe 1994 will bring me new hope!

12/14/93

The thing I'm looking forward to the most this holiday season is New Year's Day. I always loved New Year's because I go over to my friend's house and party! I don't really have any plans for New Year's or Christmas, but I'm sure they'll both be fun!

Last year, for New Year's, I went to Kristen's house (another friend) and spent the night. As soon as it was 1993, we went outside banging on pots + pans, screaming "Happy New Year!" at the top of our lungs! Maybe I'll be even more wild for the start of '94! You never know!

I have great hopes for '94. I strongly believe it will be a terrific year!

12/21/93

Naturally, I think men have it easier but, in modern civilization, I think women do. Men have to go out and earn a living to provide for their wives and families. People are usually more lenient on women because they are considered dainty and gentle; they are also considered the fairer sex.

In most cases, men have to be more responsible for their jobs, employment, lives, families, and their occupations. Women also have to be responsible, too, but not as much as men. I *am* very happy and content with being a woman; it doesn't bother me. Not to be disrespectful, but sometimes I'm glad I'm *not* a man!

1/8/94

New Year's Resolution: Jen Selinsky

My New Year's Resolution would be to become more patient. I don't try to be mean on purpose. In fact, I don't even try to be mean at all!

I sometimes have a short temper, and I get **mad** very easily. For example, if someone were to tick me off, I'd yell at them. But I'm really trying to be more patient.

When I was a child, I used to have temper tantrums all of the time. It was very disastrous. No one else in my family, that I know of, is as impatient as I. Like I said earlier, I'm really trying, and the more I try, the better I become at it.

December 1993

My favorite group is Color Me Badd. I only started to like them about 8 months ago. My favorite song at the time was "Slow Motion," but I thought it was called "All Night," and I had no idea who sang it! They also sang two other songs I had on tape, "All for Love" and "I Wanna Sex You Up." I also thought someone else sang them.

When this past November came, I literally begged my mother to go out and get their new cassette, *Time and Chance*, as a birthday present. When I first got it, I didn't know any of the new songs (except for "Time and Chance"). It took a while to get to know them, but I soon found out that this cassette contained more *romantic* songs than the last! I *love* romance; that is one of the best + most important qualities in a man! I'm now in their fan club! I just joined, but I'm sure I'll really enjoy it!

1/13/94

With half the year over, so far, I think the school year's going great. I liked this first semester a lot (even though I had too many study halls).

My two favorite classes this year are English and history. I'm glad they're all year because I don't have to leave them when I change semesters. But I'm very nervous about starting the next semester because I have hard classes + only one study hall.

This year is also much better than last year so far, I'm getting better grades and I have a better attitude. I don't know what to expect next semester, but I really liked this one!

1/24/94

As you already know, my two favorite subjects are history and English, but I'm really glad I'm in chorus. I really enjoy singing, and it's an easy credit.

Last year, I didn't even consider taking chorus (because I thought it would be boring)! I was going to take Spanish I instead, but Mr. Johns came and suggested I take chorus, instead. I put it on my schedule thinking it *would* be boring, but I was amazed when I walked in the first day! I didn't know that so many people would join. Then, I met Miss Walker for the first time. She seemed really nice, I was glad I had her as a teacher.

Right now, we are singing three songs so far "Joy to the World," "In the Mood," and "My Lord." My favorite one so far is "In the Mood." Anyway, I'm really glad I took chorus this year, and I'm considering taking it again.

1/26/94

There are a lot of things I hate, first of all, it annoys me when people don't listen and hold me back from doing my work! I also hate how people act all silly + giggly when I'm trying to concentrate on work.

I also have a lot of other pet peeves, but I don't have enough room to list them all! As I'm going to say for speech, I hate waiting. I have a whole list of things I hate waiting for, like waiting for rides at amusement parks and waiting in traffic.

My biggest pet peeve of all occurs when I'm dressed up for chorus or speech, and I have to change for stupid gym! That's another pet peeve! I'm trying to work on these pet peeves, but it'll take a while.

2/2/94

Dear Andy,

There's something I've been meaning to tell you. I'm thinking about going down to your house, just as a friend, to visit. I know you probably don't want to see me, but I really want to see you.

I think it would be great to come some Saturday in March. My mother also wants to see you, too. I think your parents would like to see us, but you'd better ask them first if we'd be allowed to come.

I also want you to know I care about you deeply, and if there's anything (or one) that is disturbing you, or if you have any problems, be sure to let me know, and I will be glad to help you through it.

Sincerely,

Jen

2/7/94

*letter for a friend assignment

One of my favorite classes this year is speech. I just started this semester, but I really like it so far. Mrs. Altemus is really nice, and she helps me get over my fear of speaking in front of people.

So far, I've had to do two speeches (intro and pet peeve.) I got an 86% on both, but I hope to do much better next time! I've also done all of my work assigned to me so far.

I have it second period every day, and in the same room (204). That's basically all I have to say so far. I'll keep you updated.

2/10/94

I think I have a great life, and I don't want to trade with anyone. There are a lot of less fortunate people in this world, and I feel bad for them, but I wouldn't want to trade lives with one of them.

There are also a lot of celebrities in this world, but I think they have difficult lives, too. They have to work all day with barely any sleep. They have no leisure time, no time for fun or families.

I just want to be the same and have the same life that I have now. I'm glad that I have this life. I may not have the best life, but I could be a lot more worse off.

2/15/94

After saving my family, I would save my tape box. It contains all of my tapes with my favorite songs on them. I would rather save my box than my radio because the radio is replaceable, and some of my tapes aren't.

Since Andy broke up with me, I listen to my music more often, but if I listen to a certain song, "Living Without Her" by C.M.B. I sometimes start to cry! Listening to music is basically all I do most of the time because there's nothing else to do. I really value my tapes, and I would die if I lost them!

2/21/94

One of my favorite foods is pizza. When I come home from school, I usually make a pizza to eat. It has been my favorite food all my life. Even though it's my favorite, there are some ingredients on it I don't even eat, like anchovies, sausage, and green peppers. The only thing I'll eat on my pizza is pepperoni.

The only kind of food I really like is Italian. Besides pizza, I like spaghetti and ravioli. I hate things like shrimp, sushi, and seafood of any kind.

Pizza is my favorite food, and it will be for a while.

2/24/94

Three things I dislike about myself are, I'm impatient, I'm lazy, and I'm also too short! The impatience and the laziness I can fix, my height I can't. I *don't* like being impatient and lazy. I'm stuck being overweight and short.

Three things I like about myself are that I can sing + draw well and that I accepted Jesus Christ as my Lord and Savior! I had an art class last semester, and I'm a first soprano in chorus. I'm also presently in Mr. Shaw's music class. I accepted Christ three years ago, and that was probably the best thing I've ever done in my life!

3/3/94

If I were to have a book of life, I wouldn't have any fancy name for it. I'd just call it *My Life*. I don't need any special name for it because it's my life, and what could be more special to me than that? Of course, I have only lived for fifteen years but, each year, I would write a chapter in my book. I would put my age and year.

I don't know if I'd ever make a book of my life but, if I did, I would be extreme and specific about it. My parents never did that, but my mother loves taking pictures, and she collects a lot of them to put in albums.

3/8/94

I love my family very much, but I also love my pet cat, April. She is very important to me, and if something were to happen to her, I don't know what I'd do.

April 2nd will be her 9th birthday, (But she'll really be 63). I got her on June of 1985, she was just a small kitten when I got her. We got her for free, but we made a $20.00 donation to the animal shelter.

She's *not* just a regular cat. She is very loyal, and she follows us around to different rooms in our house. Sometimes, she sleeps on my sister's bed, or mine.

April's really important to me, and I hope to have her around as long as she can live.

3/10/94

Some things that amuse me the most are a few of my favorite songs on the radio, like "Slow Motion," "Groove Thang," "Stay," and "Choose." After I finish my homework, I go upstairs and listen to the radio for hours.

Television amuses me a little, but not as much as it used to. I watch 2 shows on Wednesday nights, *90210* and *Melrose Place*, those are the only two shows I really watch anymore.

Also, when it's nice out, I love to ride my bike outside or take walks. Sunday, I walked up to a new housing plan, and we walked in the model home. Monday, I walked to Haine Elementary School and back. Yesterday, I just rode my bike. Those are the things that amuse me the most.

3/15/94

The ideal vacation would be to go to Florida for two months, starting April 2! I'd get away from all the jerks in this school and, by the time I get back to school, it would almost be over! I have nothing against school, in fact, I like it but, sometimes, people here tick me off!

That's not the only reason I'd like to go! I love the beautiful weather, and I could go to Disneyworld any time I choose!

California might be nice, too, but there are too many earthquakes in the Southern part.

That would be my ideal vacation, and I really would like to go there sometime.

3/20/94

I'm going to tell you a few of my top ten favorite groups and songs. Of course, my #1 favorite group is Color Me Badd, and my favorite songs of theirs in "Living Without Her." My second favorite group is Crash Test Dummies—"Hmm Hmm Hmm Hmm." My 3rd favorite is Mariah Carey—"Without You." My 4th favorite is Janet Jackson—"If." My 5th favorite is Eternal—"Stay." My 6th favorite is Aerosmith—"Living on the Edge." My 7th favorite is All-4-One—"So Much in Love." My 8th favorite is Smashing Pumpkins—"Today." My 9th favorite is Tevin Campbell—"Can We Talk." And, finally, my 10th favorite is Expose—"Never Get Over You (Getting Over Me)."

Those are some of my favorite songs and groups, I'd list more, but this is only a top 10 list!

4/6/94

Good looks and intelligence are both important to me. If I had a choice between them both, I would have to choose good looks because I could easily learn to be intelligent. It's much harder to look good than to be intelligent. But, if I had a chance to choose both, I would.

They are both important to me because both of them are really useful in life. If you wanted to be a model, you would need good looks. But if you wanted to be a scientist, you would need intelligence. But if you wanted to be a fashion designer, you would need both.

And most important, those are two good things that men look for!

4/11/94

Some of my most compulsive habits occur when I'm with my friends. I usually get nervous and bite my nails or play with my hair. I try *not* to do these things, but it doesn't work.

Also, in speech class, when I'm presenting, I tend to stand as stiff as a board. I try to give eye contact, but I'm too nervous. I can also *stutter* if I'm really nervous.

I really don't have many compulsive habits (especially gross ones). I hate having compulsive habits. I'm really trying to stop them. I don't know about you, but I think I'm doing a better job trying to stop them!

4/19/94

There are a lot of important people in my life, but the most important is my mom. She does everything for me. When I need a ride to Jen's house, she always drives me. When I'm upset or crying, my mom always comforts me. She is very sweet and generous. When I come home from school, she always has my dinner on the table, ready for me to eat, unless she's not home before me. She also helps me study for tests and with my homework if I need it. I love her very much, and she means the world to me. Sometimes, I feel as if I'm Juliet, and she's my nurse!

4/19/94

One of my most favorite times of the year is summer, even though all of the kids come out to play. I like summer because I don't have to worry about the stress of homework and going to bed early. I could sleep late and stay up all night. I also love riding my bike and getting tans. I could even exercise more and fit into my new bathing suit! I sit around all day listening to all of my favorite songs. I might even work up at that camp in Cranberry Park for the four to six-year-olds. I could also baby-sit my street neighbor, Connie, she is seven years old, and her sister's two. Her name is Tracy. I like to watch them because they are nice, and I enjoy their company. I love summertime. I wish it were summer all year long.

4/20/04

There are a lot of things I dislike about this school. First of all, some of the teachers treat us like children. I understand why, but there are some students in this school that should be treated like adults.

I also don't like some of the rules here. For example, if you are late to class three times, you get detention. I'm not saying that it's terrific to be late to class. I understand why late passes are distributed and, if the students who acted like adults were rewarded, the other students would expect the same treatment.

Again, I feel that some of the rules here are a little strict, but I understand how the school board feels about them.

5/3/94

There is nothing much that I dislike about my parents. They're both good to me. My dad may sometimes get on my nerves, (but he is a little strange). Sometimes, he jokingly makes fun of my sister, my mom, and myself. I don't think it's funny at all. He also eats everything in sight. When I get hungry, the food's all gone because of my dad. Worst of all, he walks around the house in his underwear, singing songs and making strange noises. Even though he's weird, I love him. My mother is very nice and she had a wonderful Mother's Day Sunday in Philadelphia. (I got her *Mrs. Doubtfire.*)

5/9/94

One of my favorite songs we're singing in Chorus is "Surfin' U.S.A." It's not actually the whole song, but it has a lot of other songs, including "Surfin' Safari," "Purple People Eater," "Little Surfer Girl," "Louie Louie," "The Twist," "Tutti Frutti," "Itsy Bitsy Teenie Weenie Yellow Polka Dot Bikini," and, of course, "Surfin' U.S.A." My favorite one is "Purple People Eater."

I didn't get to do the announcement for this song, but I got a speaking part.

Of all the songs we're singing, it is my favorite, and I'm sure the audience will like it too because it's one of the best songs.

5/12/94

Some good ideas for journal topics would be "What I Thought About English Class This Year," "My Future Plans for College," "Ideal Mate," "My Favorite Class," "What Is a Value You Would Fight for?," and "If You Could Choose an Age for the Rest of Your Life, How Old Would You Be?"

Those are just my opinions, anyone could think of their own topics. I also have a lot more that I can't list because they're too many.

I enjoyed writing journals this year because it has helped me improve my writing skills, and I could express how I really feel.

I don't know about anyone else, but I really enjoyed this experience, and I hope it will last a lifetime.

5/17/94

I really don't have any plans for summer vacation. I might just stay home and to go the Sheraton to swim. Hopefully, I'll go somewhere this summer and not stay home the whole time.

I'm going to exercise a lot and lie out to get more tan. (I'm trying to lose weight so I could fit into a bikini.) My sister has an aerobic step block, I usually turn on the radio and step to the music. I also do sit-ups and ride my bike to the music. I used to go to a tanning bed at the Hair Gallery, but since the sun's out more often, I just lie out in the sun.

That's about all I really have planned. Hopefully, that's not all I *am* going to do.

5/19/94

One of my favorite books is *The Secret Garden*. I first heard of it five years ago in my 4th grade elementary school class, our teacher would read us a chapter or two a day. Also, at the end of the year, we saw the movie. I thought it was a very interesting book, and I thought the movie was great, too.

About a year later, I saw the movie again, (but I think it was a different version). Another version of the movie just came out recently. I never got to see it, but it looked good.

I never thought I'd get to read the book again but, when I saw it on sale at the book fair, I knew I was going to buy it.

I hope I will be able to buy it soon so I can enjoy it time and time again.

5/25/94

I've learned a lot this past year. From Miss Walker (my chorus director), I've learned how to breathe properly and the correct singing posture. From Mrs. Altemus, I've learned how to deliver speeches correctly and a few organs of the body that produce sound. From Mr. Donnelly, I learned a few art techniques. From Mrs. Simoff, I learned how to type and how to work a typing computer. From Mrs. Vrana, I leaned pre-algebra. From Mrs. Booker + Mr. Lutz, I learned about the weather and astronomy. From Mrs. Gilliland, I learned how important physical fitness is and how to play a few sports. From Mr. Shaw, I learned about The Beatles and other famous groups. From Mr. Perkins, I learned about the American Revolution and the Civil War. And from Mrs. Wise + you, I leaned a little more about grammar and the wonderful novels we read in our literature book. Your class was really enjoyable, and I hope to continue to write stories. I hope you had as much fun this year as I did. I will always remember you. Good luck and God bless!

5/20/94

I've never really been tan most of my life, until I went to the Hair Gallery. It was about two months ago when I had to get my hair cut. My sister's friend, Amy Forte, mentioned there was also a tanning bed there, so I decided to try it. I made my first appointment for the following Monday, and I loved it. Now, I've been going ever since.

I don't know if I'll do it next summer, but I have appointments every Wednesday for the rest of this month. I also lie out at the pool, or in my backyard.

I stay in the tanning booth for 1 half hour per day, and I go twice a week. (Monday + Wednesday.)

I'm glad Amy told me about the tanning bed because I think it's nice to be tan for once in my life.

6/2/94

Monday 11/22/93

Mrs. McKinley,

My name's Jen Selinsky, and I am fifteen years old. My hobbies are listening to music and riding my bike. My favorite food is pizza. I also like going to the Sheraton to swim for exercise.

I also love to listen to music. My favorite group is Color Me Badd! My favorite song of theirs is "Groovy Now."

My family consists of four people and one cat. My sister's name is Amy. She is twenty. She goes to college and is majoring in business. My dad's name is Robert, and he works for the Pillsbury Company. My mother's name is Toni. She used to be a substitute teacher, but she quit last year when she had back surgery. My cat's name is April because she was born on April 2.

I have a boyfriend named Andy. He is sixteen and he lives in Upper Marlboro, Maryland. He plays football and baseball + he also wrestles. Well, that's about all.

Right now, I would rather be at Andy's house. I have so much fun when I go up there! I really enjoy talking to him and his family; he has a mother + father, and two younger sisters named Sara and Amy.

Sometimes, we go up to his bedroom and play video games or listen to music. His house is really new and fancy, my favorite room is the dining room because it is really pretty.

He lives in a real nice plan. Sometimes, Andy and I go for walks and look at all the houses. Like his, all of the houses are really pretty. So that's where I'd like to be right now!

12/3/93

Something happened this weekend that I was very sad about, Andy and I broke up! We didn't have a fight, but he said we lived too far apart from each other. (He lives in Maryland.)

I cried most of Saturday night when he told me; he was sad, too. I was even sadder when I had to leave him for the last time.

The next day, I came home at about 5:00 and got ready for youth group, but I didn't really have much fun because I was still sad.

A while later, my friend Shawna, came up to me and asked me what was wrong. I told her everything, and she felt sorry for me.

I called her last night, and she said she has a friend in 10th grade that needed a girlfriend. I hate fix-ups, but maybe this one just might work.

12/7/93

I, Jen Selinsky, spent my summer doing lots of things. First of all, I went to Maryland to see my boyfriend. We had a lot of fun together. First of all, we went to see one of his baseball games. His team won fifteen to one. Then, we went back to his house for a cookout and after that his father took both of us to see *Hot Shots Part Deux*. I thought it was very funny! After the movie, I went back to his house for a while but, soon after, I had to go back to my grandparents' to spend the night.

For the next week or so, I basically just stayed home and rode my bike or went out with my friends. Sometimes, we went to the mall or the movies. The first movie I saw the summer with my friends was *Made in America*. I thought that it was very good, too!

The last two or three weeks of June, I started to help watch the children up at day camp in Cranberry Park. I liked working up there because I got a chance to meet some of the people and help children with the crafts and activities! I joined up for a membership to swim there year round. Camp lasted until the beginning of August.

The week of August 4, Andy came down to our house for three days. One day, we went to Kennywood and, the next day, we saw *Jurassic Park*. Saturday, the 7th, we took him back to Maryland.

One week later, we went to Cedar Point for the day. It was really fun but, since the park was big, we didn't have time to go on all the rides. My favorite ride was the Mean Streak, one of the biggest roller coasters there.

Finally, August 22, I saw Andy for the last time this summer. I went down to his house for the day and spent the night at Lynn's house. (She is my mother's friend.)

In conclusion, I'd like to say I had fun. It was really an interesting summer, and it was the best one yet.

I must admit that English 102 is one of the last courses I've taken to obtain my associate's degree, but it has definitely been worthwhile, and I am glad that I saved one of the best for last.

Every Thursday night, I looked forward to attending the course, even though the commute from Cranberry Township was long. I have always been intent upon class participation, and I am more than eager to put in my two cents.

My classmates were likeable and helpful, as we worked together and shared our writings with each other. I couldn't have asked for a more cooperative crew.

As I mentioned in another document, the readings were enjoyable, as well as proactive. I found myself having an easy time reading them as I did commenting on and analyzing them. The journal assignments were a fun part of the class because we got to respond to them, ourselves, and have others add to our comments! That was one of the most enjoyable parts of the class.

Again, the group work coincides with what I just mentioned because that was part of the journal assignments. I would also like to restate that my classmates were kind and fun to work with, who could ask for someone better?

I would now like to thank Mr. Robert Dandoy for being such a wonderful and helpful instructor. His words of constructive criticism and encouragement have helped me through the course, and I don't think I could have experienced anyone more congenial and cooperative than him. He strove to have us do our best, and he was successful (at least, in my case).

He managed his time properly, and gave us each all the guidance that we needed. I appreciated being able to reach him by home when I had a question.

Mr. Dandoy also reassured us that we would have no problem with the course if we did what he asked of us in a timely manner. And, as his student, that information was very helpful.

Last, but not least, I'd like to comment on the class as a whole, which was basically defined in the paragraphs above.

I feel it was a good course, one of the best that I have had at the college. I am glad to have taken it as one my final choices, and I hope that many students, in the future, will enjoy the course as much as I did.

12/4/99

Like some lucky people, I have had (and still do) a wonderful relationship with my parents. My father is a caring and loving man, who has never once doubted my abilities, or me, and he's given all the support, to my sister and I, that we needed.

As much as I love my father, I find myself being closer to my mother. She has given me everything, and she is everything.

The two of us, so to speak, are "intertwined." It is extremely difficult for either of us to live without the other. We have built a common bond of trust for one another. My mother is my mentor.

My older sister and I are approximately five years apart, so our relationship has never been that close. As children, we'd fight and quarrel. It seemed as if the two of us were naturally pitted against each other. Growing up, we found ourselves having many differences, with a few similarities split amongst us. And we still do!

For example, I love to read, and she hates it. She is physically hard-working, and I am not. The only things we seem to have in common are our parents and genders.

Lately, however, I have found our relationship growing closer because she was recently engaged. I tend to share the joy with her. We're growing and getting on with our lives.

I am originally from Cranberry Township, and I still live there to this day. Just as many others, I grew up in a middle class home. My mother worked as a substitute teacher, until I reached the age of twelve, earning the going rate for substitutes, which at the end was about $50.00 per day. My father worked as a sales representative for the Pillsbury Company for thirty years. However, he recently retired, so now we're going to be as poor as church mice! His income was not extraordinarily high, but he seemed to take home a decent amount, being that we are (or were) middle class constituents.

My family's expectations for my sister and I were not the highest, but they are pleased with our accomplishments. My mother and father were primarily concerned about our happiness and well-being, just as any good parents should have been.

Now that I am enrolled in college and am about to obtain my AA degree in humanities, my parents, especially my mother, have higher expectations of me. And I believe that is good because I know that she cares about my education. That means a lot to me.

Another very important being in my life is my pet cat, April. This may sound a little awkward, but she comforts me when I feel upset. It's almost as if I had a daughter of my own. My "baby girl," as I call her, knows when I'm upset, and she approaches me. I start to gently stroke her fur, and I feel relaxed.

Just to hear her purr melts my heart. I love having her rub her head against my hand for love and attention, and it is a treat to have her sleep with me every night. She feels almost like a live teddy bear when I hold her in my arms. I don't know what I'd do without her.

My school experience was similar to that of a typical dork. I was picked on and called all kinds of names, but this was only during junior high. But I had my fair share of acceptance, especially during my senior year. I had joined various clubs, such as the Art Club and the Library Literary Club.

My senior year, I was vice president of the latter. Now that I look back on it, I wish that I would have taken my academics more seriously.

Come graduation, I pulled through with almost a 3.0 GPA. Unfortunately, the classes in which I excelled carried less weight than those I didn't do so well in. But I am the only one who's somewhat dismayed with my academic experience.

I was not in the popular crowd in high school. In my junior high years, the fact that I wasn't with the "in crowd" slightly bothered me. But, during my senior high years, it fazed me much less. Everyone had his or her little clique, and I obviously didn't fit in, but that gave me a great sense of individuality.

I was my own person, and I still am. It was not as if I didn't have any friends, because I did, and they were those of who didn't fit in much either. We were the individualists.

As many other adolescents, I have had my successes and failures, and most of my high school grades are examples of both. I was always good at English and the humanities. Between the ages of fourteen and eighteen, I had had five official publications. They have made me proud and have given me a sense of accomplishment. As for my failures, they were definitely outweighed by my successes (I didn't have anything special to achieve in mathematics) and the only effect that they've had on me was a small feeling of regret.

I wish that I could go back in time and turn those Cs and Ds into As and Bs. My high school grade point average is the only negative effect that my failures have had, and it's all that they ever will.

Of course, my parents were (and still are) influential. But some of my high school teachers have influenced me the most. I remember one in particular, Miss Schaudt, who had inspired me to become a writer.

Sure, I'd written things before the tenth grade, by many of those compositions were strictly for previous school assignments. But she grabbed a hold of me and taught me to write with my heart, as well as my mind, and, to this day, I have not forgotten what she has done for me.

Another influential part of my adolescence was the combination of poetry and rock music. And, for those who don't know to what I am referring, I am referring to the musical group, The Doors, Jim Morrison, in particular. His poetry has inspired me to write and think. His words moved me to my independence.

Without Morrison's brilliance, I probably wouldn't have found my true talent for poetry. He is my intellectual muse, and he shall remain to be just that as long as I live.

At the age of fourteen, I had my first official boyfriend and, between then and now, I have had plenty. Being that I've had numerous boyfriends, I've had the experience of dating along with it.

And I believe that all these experiences were good because each of them has taught me something, whether it's how to please members of the opposite gender, or how to please myself.

Too many people, these days, either get into, or stay, in relationships that aren't satisfying, just for the sake of having someone. I'd rather be alone and content than to be in an unpleasant relationship.

Oftentimes, people tend to stay with the first person they date. The problem with that is that those people lack the experience of dating other people. And that experience is virtually essential for finding the "perfect person."

The "facts of life" are taught at different times in different families. The school systems also play a part in presenting the information about sexuality. My first exposure to the "facts of life" was probably around the age of ten.

At that time, I had no interest in the subject. In fact, I thought it was inappropriate and gross to mention. But I later learned that this information is important.

Many people learn misinformation from their peers, so that is why it's important to depend on a reliable source for such information. I imagine that many teen pregnancies, and the spreading of STDs, are results of such misinformation.

My role as a woman, described by some, is probably different from what it would have been forty years ago. I don't have to cook, clean, marry, or have children nowadays (according to society), and I can definitely speak my mind. Today's society strongly encourages the fifth, but it encourages the first four as well.

Cooking and cleaning are good skills for both men and women to have (even though I don't do them).

As for the latter two, they are completely my choice as to whether or not I want to do them, and I don't.

Being the woman that I am, I have every right to do most anything that men can do. I've abolished all the sexist stereotypes in my mind, and I have made myself into the person that I am.

I find myself to be an open-minded person when it comes to members of the opposite sex. To be frank, I love men. They treat me with such respect and kindness.

In fact, the majority of my friends are male. I do have my fair share of female friends, and they are kind to me as well, but they don't really fulfill my emotional needs. When something is ailing me, or when I just want to tell of my wonderful day, it is the men that I turn to for conversation, not the women.

Men just always seem more congenial and less wiling to stab me in the back, so to speak. I can easily be myself around men, and it's just the opposite with women. With the male gender, I find myself having no envy. There is, however, an unspoken, unexpressed jealousy (for the most part) when it comes to other women. I would rather all the man pay attention to me. Very few people know this for a fact, but one could easily detect it.

I would like to take a few sentences to introduce another very special person in my life, my wonderful boyfriend, Gene. He is a prime example, of love, for me. Next to my mother, he treats me the best of anyone I know (and his looks don't hurt, either).

Gene is the most kind, understanding, and sympathetic person I have encountered. Aside from me, he treats his family and friends wonderfully. And I don't think that I could have asked God to create me a better "significant other."

My goals, for the most part, have not yet been achieved. I am still working on two or three very important things in my life. The first two pertain to my education after Butler County Community College, and they are to attend Clarion University to earn a BA in English and an MLS in library science.

It will be at least a few more years until I achieve these goals. The third pertains to a leisure activity, my poetry. Before I depart this earth, I aspire to write more than 1,800 poems. The renowned poet, Emily Dickinson, has been famed for writing that much. So far, I have close to nine books completed for a total of approximately 1,600 poems. And, if I hurry, I shall achieve that goal within the next few months.

As stated earlier, I chose the career of a librarian. And I believe that it was a good choice because I love to read, and I love to be surrounded by books. Call me crazy, but the sheer atmosphere just tickles my fancy. Some aspects, such as shelving books, may sound like a time-consuming process, and it is, but it's all the more worthwhile. Besides, I don't think there's any other career that I can tolerate as much!

As for my adequacies and inadequacies, I feel, unfortunately, that they are equal. On the optimistic side, I know that I can perform fairly well in the arts, being that I am able to paint, draw, write, sing, and do well in certain sciences. I also project a decent amount of common sense when it comes to many things.

However, I feel inadequate when it comes to subjects such as mathematics and computer science. Even though those skills are slowly improving, I still feel that I am unable to perform well in those areas because some of my peers (and those from other age groups) seem to be better able to perform such tasks.

I believe that I am, for the most part, open-minded and flexible. Some people may irk me more than others, but I tend to keep my cool in most frustrating situations. The position in which I work requires me to deal with the public, and I am requested to keep my temper under control. A few years in the past, I probably wouldn't have been able to do what I do now. Over the last few years, I have gained more patience, and it has enabled me to expand my flexibility.

In the paragraphs preceding this one, I have mentioned a few people who have influenced me, my parents, Miss Schaudt, Jim Morrison, but I could always add some more to the list. Others who have inspired me include Emily Dickinson, Mark Twain, Helen Keller, Martin Luther King Jr., Maya Angelou, René Descartes, Wolfgang Amadeus Mozart, Johann Sebastian Bach, Richard Wagner, and Sojurner Truth.

They have influenced me to write, to sing, to philosophize, and to stand up for my own beliefs. I sometimes wonder what my life would be like if it weren't for the influence of these people, but I'm glad that I don't have to wonder too much. Their existence and actions all happened for a reason, and I'm glad to know that they have affected history today.

Something else that has influenced me to do what I do is the idea of human equality. Even though some people may not have the same strengths as others, God created everyone to be equal. One thing that infuriates me the most about the issue is discrimination. Not only am I referring to racial discrimination, but I am referring to the discrimination of religion and gender as well. Shouldn't we have learned from our mistakes centuries ago? Shouldn't we have taken the time to educate ourselves? If not, there's no better time to start than now. Education can make a whole world of difference.

My present position in life entails me being a full-time student at the Butler County Community College and a part-time worker at the Carmike Cinemas in Cranberry. And, even though my job is important for earning wages, I put much more time and effort into my schoolwork.

According to many of those in my life, I tend to downgrade myself much of the time. Since I know and I have come into contact with those who are more talented, more intelligent, and better looking than me, I feel inadequate as an individual.

This may seem a little pretentious, but if I'm not the best at what I do, I feel as if I'm nothing. The green-eyed monster rears its ugly head. But how others see me is sheer flattery. They see me as a beautiful, intelligent woman, who should be proud of her accomplishments. And they don't understand why I tend to cut myself down. Perhaps it's a cry for attention; perhaps it's a way to escape.

I feel I communicate very well with those I know. I am very blunt in telling people my feelings and thoughts. Perhaps, sometimes, I am too blunt. But my points get across easier that way. However, when someone offends me, I find it hard to tell him or her.

I am exceedingly afraid of hurting someone's feelings. I've been told that I need to be honest in that area of communication. Maybe, someday, I'll learn to put my emotions first.

My value system, most importantly, includes those of whom I love dearly. I take pride in my friends and family, and I'll go out of my way to protect them from harm.

Second on this list is education. I take pride in what I learn, and I look forward to my future lessons.

And, thirdly, I take pride in my beliefs. I stick to them no matter the circumstance. They define my life and personality.

I see myself as an easy person with which to get along, and I'd say that my relationships with others are meaningful and worthwhile. As I mentioned in a previous paragraph, I tend to get along with men easier than women.

Their personalities are much more interesting to me. I can act like myself around them, and I don't have to wear a fraudulent mask. My relationships with others are fair only because I know to set aside time for myself. (I sometimes like to be alone.) And, if that weren't the case, I'd drive myself crazy.

My view of a meaningful occupation is one that keeps me satisfied, no matter the circumstance(s). My wages and income don't matter so much, as long as I am otherwise fulfilled. Why should I bother to do something that I dislike on a daily basis? That wouldn't be meaningful and, if it's not meaningful, it's not worthwhile. What's expected of me is obvious. I am to put forth 100% every day. And, if the job is worthwhile, I will do just that. Both the yin and the yang are needed to make a full balance.

If I do what's mentioned above, my chances for success are greater than if I don't do the stated. If I set my mind to a goal, I can achieve it. Nothing can stop an optimistic attitude. It also depends on how one defines success. One can be rich, but unsatisfied. Another can be poor, but content. It all depends on the definition.

I have no immediate plans for marriage in the near future. In fact, I don't think that it's all that necessary. One can be in love, and that could be enough to satisfy an individual. What are a few vows and a set of precious metals to signify? I've also been told that marriage can destroy love, if it's done half-heartedly. I'm definitely not ready to get married, and I don't think I will be for a few more years down the road.

As I mentioned earlier, gender roles do not affect me because I do not pay attention to them. I just do whatever I feel is right, be that whether it's considered a traditional female role or not.

Gender should not determine a person's intelligence or ability, for gender should be respected. Men cannot live without women, and women cannot live without men. That's the way God meant for it to be, and that's how it's going to be. Plain and simple.

When it comes to what I need from members of the opposite gender, it would be best described as emotional. I'm a very sensitive person, and I require a lot of love and attention. If a man cannot meet my emotional needs, then he is no good for me. I must have someone who is sympathetic and understanding in order for me to feel that my needs have been fulfilled.

I view the good life as a life in which I am financially secure, but I don't have to work very hard to get there. I want to enjoy every minute of the time I spend doing the things that I love. I want to love and be loved in return. I want my knowledge to be constantly expanding so that when my number comes up, people will look back and see how much I knew. I want to be close to my idea of perfection.

I will achieve these goals by doing the best that I can in all my areas of strength (and weakness). It all depends on the timing and the circumstance(s). I don't have to work hard to achieve all these goals, but I do for some of them.

My value system corresponds to these plans in that I plan to be surrounded by loving friends and family, and the Lord, most of all! That is what I value the most, and I plan for them to remain in my life. I also place a high value on education. And I definitely need that in order to live a good life. It's interesting how all these aspects correspond.

The good life is related to my chosen occupation because I want to have a job that I enjoy. And, if I don't enjoy it, then my life won't be complete. It's as simple as that.

My priorities for the future include having organization, goals, and a good attitude. Pessimism is oblivion. Also, to get me through, I need a good mind, which will enable me to make the right decisions and have a few regrets. A good conscience is required in order for me to have the clear mind, which will help me make sense of those decisions.

And, most importantly, I need my faith in God, Who has helped me (through so many ordeals in my time of need). I am grateful for the gift of salvation through the blood of Christ!

I like to be alone some of the time, but a few good relationships are needed in order for me to be happy. One can never have too many friends, for they are virtually essential for getting one through life.

I plan to do this by staying open-minded and having good social skills. If I want to meet new people, I can't be shy and introverted. I must be willing to open up. And if I don't, it'll just be more difficult for me to fraternize.

As I have mentioned in the previous paragraphs, I have no immediate plans for marriage. Neither my boyfriend, nor I, are ready for it. (At least not now.)

The way that I see it, to share my life with Gene (or anyone else, for that matter) would be a burden, even though I'd love him. I need time for myself, and I feel that marriage would jeopardize that and my love for my man.

If I were to get married, my responsibilities would be to love, honor, and cherish the person. I would have no problem with that, but it's the sacrifices that require me to draw the line. I don't mind compromise, but I won't hinder my beliefs, or time, in order for a marriage to function. Call me selfish, if you like.

For the same hypothetical circumstance, I would expect my family and friends to respect the decision I made and the man whom I choose to marry. They don't, however, have to like or appreciate the decision I made. But I do expect the support from others in what I choose to do, and that is all I require.

Last, but not least, my biggest problem (or problem) will be overcoming my laziness. I am not referring to academic laziness, (as one can plainly see from the length of my document) but I am referring to physical sloth.

My older sister obtained the hard-working gene, but not I. But by laziness, my physical appearance, and my outlook on life will both change for the worse.

This may not pose as much of a threat now as it will be in the future, because I am currently living at home. Ten years from now, that may not be the circumstance (or, at least, I hope so). Nobody likes too much physical work or, at least, I don't.

Basically, I am referring to housework and all that is required to keep a household running smoothly, such as cooking, shopping, cleaning, laundry and the like. These are just not things that I enjoy. But I realize that they are a necessary *evil* if I am to live on my own, or with an eventual spouse.

1/25/00

Last Tuesday evening, I had the privilege of meeting and having supper with Ann Pancake. I especially like the fact that the meeting was held in Davis Hall, rather than Moore Hall. The atmosphere was much more welcoming, and I felt as if I was talking to a professor with whom I was very familiar.

Unfortunately, for occupational reasons, I had to miss Ms. Pancake's actual reading, but the discussion was really interesting. I got to find out some personal information about the author, such as where she grew up and what kinds of writers inspired her. She even told us that her surname, Pancake, was very common in many parts of West Virginia. There was also a brief discussion about a distant relative of hers who was also a famed writer.

As I implied in a previous paragraph, the formality of Moore Hall prevented me from asking more questions of the two other visiting writers, (Mr. Drayer and Mr. Gibb). Having the meeting in Davis Hall made me feel otherwise. I felt more at home, and I felt more important because I was comfortable with myself.

The most enjoyable part, for me, was getting to talk to Ms. Pancake after the formal part of the discussion. She even gave me her autograph and agreed to let me take her picture. Ms. Pancake seemed impressed with the amount I had written, and she encouraged me to stick to my aspirations of becoming a writer, no matter what criticism I may encounter. She is an impressive writer and an interesting person, and I hope to purchase her book when it gets published. I would also like to see her again sometime in the near future.

11/14/00

Humor in Writing

Truly, I believe that there are many incidents that can make a particular piece of literature very humorous.

What I seem to find pretty hilarious is irony, (but not all). In a certain story or poem, when something is the precise opposite of what I expected, I find that funny.

There are also other sources of entertainment, besides writings; (such as music and television) they almost always seem to have different ways to express humorous things or incidents. Mainly, though, I want to direct my emphasis to the ironic humors that many writers possess, and contain in their literature. Nothing seems to make me laugh any faster. Sarcasm is another, but it seems more common to me on television.

So, basically, the main point I want to emphasize is that irony is "the mother of all humor."

2/21/96

How to Act if Your House Is Attacked by Foreigners

Well, if a particular American family lives in the city of Verona, Italy, that would certainly make them foreign. (Though, that is besides the point.)

If that particular American family is enjoying a Sunday afternoon in their Italian hotel, when suddenly, angry men burst in with the bloody red faces, it is not correct for any family member to scream bloody murder and run around naked in panic.

Those angry Italian men come in screaming. "Mussolini, hail Mussolini!"

If it is not in the early 1940s, it would be improper to say, "World War II is over—hello!" You should react nicely.

"Oh," the wife/mother replied. "Look at this, some Italian men have come to visit."

"Yes," the husband/father replied. "We should offer them your world famous pasta."

The angry mob had puzzled expressions on their faces. "Pasta, world famous?"

"Oh, yes," the mother said. "You simply must try it."

The bewildering experience has caused the men to start revolting again. They didn't want to wait for their dinner like civilized people. Besides, all the fighting would only help increase their appetites.

The family did not like all the fighting; they were simply appalled that these men were still carrying on like this.

The Mrs. then heard the noise and started to scold. "Shame on you, making all that ruckus in this hotel."

The four men were then demanding to rob the place.

Father overheard this and was overjoyed. "Here, men, have forty ducats of ours!"

"More, more!" They angrily demanded.

"Sure, have this lamp, and our bedroom sheets!"

This angered the wife, for she planned to "use" them later.

"Children, go set the table," she demanded.

They merrily skipped over the kitchen area.

"And you can have those, too, if you gentlemen wish!" the father exclaimed.

The table was set, and the pasta was complete.

"Oh, boys," the mother cried. "Soup's on."

"Soup?" one asked in bewilderment.

Well, basically, the four got angry until the first bite of pasta was tasted.

Then, a feeling of nausea entered, which caused the four men to drown themselves in the rivers of Venice, and they were never to be heard from again.

The pasta was then "world famous" in the use of preventing crime in countries all across the globe.

1996

Valuable Amenities

One of the most valuable things, to me, is my intelligence. (There are others that correspond to that.) For instance; I like to have a lot of reading and writing activities in use for my leisure time. There is a whole bookshelf in my room that contains over fifty books. (I have not read them all yet, but I will eventually.)

For my writing activities; I am presently writing a few stories, (alternating from one to another) but, so far, they are brief. Poetry is great, too! I have some artistic and musical interests as well.

A few years back (in the junior high) I have won a few awards for my work. Also, some were entered in art shows, but my work has improved drastically over the course of a few years.

I am also presently in the Seneca Valley Girls' Chorus group with Mrs. Latagliata. (I would rather be in a more prestigious group.) This summer, I will be entering the Cranberry Choir, but I will be the youngest member.

If I have to give any of these up, I would have no idea what the significance of my life would be. Every day,

I dwell on these subjects (also with other interests on my mind) as if they were the most important in the whole world. It is also mentioned that I bring these subjects up <u>too</u> much.

My mother wishes that I was a bit more "normal" for my age, and it is true that I have different (or opposite) thoughts (and beliefs) than others.

If this were different, I would have a fantastic void in my vast mind and heart. Thoughts of melancholy; death would constantly roll through my mind. As Mark Twain in his "Carnival of Crimes" story, I could be conscience-laden. Possibly, I would have anxiety attacks galore!

This whole entry, itself, may sound a tad drastic, but <u>this</u> is how I would truly feel if I would ever have to give up these wonderful activities any time during my life.

3/29/96

The junior high and intermediate high schools are similar in many ways. They're both located in the same place, that's very helpful for all people who attend. Both principals seem to be fair and understanding. I also like the basic setup of these buildings. They're designed very nicely.

These buildings are also different in many ways too. For example, the intermediate building is much larger. It seems hard to find your way at first. But things get better every day. Also, in the Intermediate building we have social study halls! And, last, but not least the Intermediate building has a better system. You get treated like an adult. That's my favorite!

My favorite of the two buildings is, of course, the intermediate high school. I absolutely love being treated like an adult. It's a real privilege! I can't stand being treated like an immature little seventh grader! Social study halls are terrific. They allow you to talk to your friends. I love the Intermediate building, and I'm really glad to be here!

9/15/94

Swing. Swing. Swing. Love. Love. Love. The beginning of the groovy times. Rock 'n' roll and the Vietnam War. I'm talking about the '60s and early '70s, man! Known as the "Ruby Age." A time of war and violence, but also that of peace and love.

The Vietnam War broke out in the late '60s, and men were drafted into the armed services. The recruits were conservative and very straight-laced. They were ordered around by commanders and ordered to hate and kill. "A bunch of slaves!" as the hippies called them.

People in the Army hated hippies, hated the love generation. They thought all the killing and violence was "helping protect the country from foreign invaders." Their brainwashed intelligence came in handy just for more killing and violence.

The hippies, the peacemakers, the flower children wanted world peace. "There's no need for fighting, and violence. Why can't we just get along?" Intellectually inclined the hippies wanted to be. "The golden age has returned, live it. Love one another. Love animals, love, love, love. Let's not return to the Iron Age, which was worthless!"

Hippies wanted to be heard, not discriminated against. Great bands also formed, such as The Beatles, The Doors, The Grateful Dead, and Pink Floyd. They inspired people who wanted to listen. Unlike The Beatles, The Grateful Dead were pretty obscure.

In the early '70s some groupies for The Grateful Dead, called Deadheads, followed them around the country on tours. They, too, wanted to be one.

The '60s and early '70s were fabulous times never to be forgotten. (I myself would like to have been a hippie.) No generation could ever hold a candle to the Ruby Age.

1/9/95

Dicso, alternative, rap, you guessed it. Time for the late '70s, '80s, and '90s, baby! A fine time to be alive. New technologies blooming up from under our noses! An exciting birth for the new generation, the "Emerald Age."

In the late '70s the "hippie thing" was pretty much over. In the year 1977, disco became popular. It was a certain kind of dance music. Also, people in leisure suits danced on these lighted boards. There really was no purpose or bonding. People just got drunk and partied. (Thank God I wasn't born 'til the following year.)

Nothing much happened in the rest of the decade, so on to the '80s. Two terrible things I recall happening, gangs and AIDS. There were gangs decades before, but they just got worse in the '80s. More violence and drugs. This is a problem in today's society, which needs to be fixed.

The other thing is AIDS, which stands for Acquired Immune Deficiency Syndrome. HIV is a condition that eventually leads to AIDS. It's caused by unprotected sex, or sharing needles. The virus attacks your T cells, which are linked to the immune system. There is presently no vaccine, or cure, so therefore the result is death.

In the mid '80s more technologies emerged suddenly. Computers have become more advanced, top brands included IBM and Apple Macintosh. They were formed into smaller sizes and uses of keyboards. Also, CDs came around in 1985. They were said to be better than vinyl, or cassettes—a compact disc that is shaped like a record and is ten times more efficient.

Music in the '80s was pretty good. The start of alternative music, played by people formally known as college bands—groups such as R.E.M. and Nirvana. They were obscure until they appeared on the radio and MTV. In the late '80s rap came out, but let's not get into that!

In the early '90s even *more* technologies emerged (also which dealt with computers and CDs).

The Emerald Age is like another Industrial Revolution in the spreading of new technologies. In the near future, almost every job will require a computer skill of some kind.

Also, unfortunately, crime has gotten worse this decade. It is more violent and gang dominated. President Clinton is trying to reach out to people. "Stop the violence! It's not worth risking the lives of our youth and our country. Peace, live it, or rest in it!" The passing of ages, over generations, is an example of how corrupt and intelligent people have become. I hope, by the year 2000, this violence will come to an end.

1/9/95

12/4/99

Sara Brigance, Esq.

1201 Fifth Avenue

Suite #203

Pittsburgh, PA.

15087

Mr. Robert Dandoy:

My name is Sara Brigance, and I am a lawyer representing the case of good writing documents.

In this briefcase, I submit evidence in the form of documents (labeled exhibit a through H) to you, the private jury, I would hope that you would acquit my client, Jen Selinsky, from the clutches me mediocrity. Then, hopefully, you will render your verdict that will proclaim the body of writings to be of excellent quality.

For further instructions, please make sure to check the front and back pages of all journals and processed drafts.

All the requirements are there. Please follow the instructions accordingly to make your judgment on the merits of the different exhibits. Your time and effort is very much appreciated.

Thank you.

Sincerely,

Sara Brigance

The portfolio, in my opinion, was a good experience for me to have. Not only did I have the opportunity for extra credit, but I got to use my creativity as well. I am also grateful for the early announcement of the project; that enabled me to get an early start on my writing assignments.

Even though we had little discussion on the journals, I still enjoyed the fact that we were encouraged to give our opinions on the writings. It was also a good idea to have us write little comments, on separate pages, as to what we read. That helped me to focus better on the different journal entries and understand them better.

The whole concept of the research paper was not entirely new, as I have done in some high school English courses. This college experience has enabled me to be more effective in my writing because the sources had to be cited, and we were able to use the MLA format. The length was good, and I had enough room to write about many aspects of my topic.

The constructive criticism I received on my processed drafts was excellent because it persuaded me to narrow my topics and focus more on the subject. The grades I received were legitimate and fair. I worked many hours on the documents, and I could only improve with revision.

The assignment, as a whole, was excellent because it enabled me to use my full potential on the assigned work and to expand my creativity. I am exceedingly grateful for such a well-balanced and comprehensive opportunity to learn and improve. I am sure that it also challenged and inspired the other students as well. I hope that, in the near future, I will be doing another project such as this, and I'm sure that, by assigning the portfolio early, other students will have the same opportunity as we did to use their full potential on the portfolio. This is one of the best classroom opportunities that I have ever received.

12/4/99

Contributions

The positive contributions I plan to make during the class may be considered standard, but they are positive, nonetheless. I will do my best to show up on time and devote all my attention to what's being studied or discussed. I will never be the cause of any distractions that allow the students or the professor to feel uncomfortable.

As all my attention will be focused on the material covered in class, I'll do my best to have prepared and correct answers for any questions given to me. I will also state my answers to the best that my knowledge will allow me so that the professor has a good understanding as to where I stand on a certain text or issue.

Along with the contributions I listed above, I shall give full and accurate opinions on any (and all) the material to be covered. If I'm not particularly fond of a certain text or issue, I will be honest in saying so. I see no point in lying to make myself sound better in the classroom, and I wish that many others would share this view with me. These are the things that I promise to do, and they will certainly have a positive outcome with everyone concerned.

1/22/01

Final Grade

The grade that I expect to receive in this course is an A, and I can justify by stating many reasons. First of all, I have made it to each and every class period this semester. Even though I was late on some occasions, I had a legitimate reason for being so, because I was held up in my last class.

I sat through all the lectures and gave all my interest to the subjects brought up. I can clearly say that I was never the cause of any distraction, and I did not inflict any discomfort by being impolite or crass.

I admit that I did not participate as much as some of the other students, but I made it a point to contribute at least once every class period.

The answers that I gave to the corresponding questions were honest and stated to the best of my knowledge. Along with the verbal participation, I made sure that I had cards written out and turned in for every day of my attendance.

I gave my opinion on all the material covered. If I was not fond of a certain idea or issue, I informed the professor and the others students. I also contributed some ideas of my own. Well, it's been a great semester, and a whole new world of literature was opened up to me. I'd like to thank you for your time and support, and I hope to have another of your classes in the future.

5/9/01

About the Author

Jen Selinsky was born in 1978 in Pittsburgh, PA. She was raised in Cranberry Township. In December 2004, Jen earned her MLS from Clarion University of Pennsylvania. She now lives in Sellersburg, IN with her husband.

Some of Jen's short works have been published in several anthologies, including *The Raider Review*, *Tobeco*, and *Essence of a Dream*, published by The National Library of Poetry—for which her poem, "Ode to the Forest," won an editor's choice award.

www.ingramcontent.com/pod-product-compliance
Lightning Source LLC
Chambersburg PA
CBHW051230130726
47988CB00001B/292